table of Contents

Ray Pritchard

is president of Keep Believing Ministries, a dynamic organization that includes a national preaching ministry and other good-will efforts. For 26 years he pastored churches in Los Angeles, Dallas, and Chicago. He has written a number of popular books, including *The Leadership Lessons of Jesus* (with Bob Briner; B&H Publishing Group). Dr. Pritchard and his wife have three grown sons and live in Tupelo, Mississippi.

master*Work:*
Essential Messages from God's Servants

• Designed for developing and maturing believers who desire to go deeper into the spiritual truths of God's Word.

• Ideal for many types of Bible study groups.

• A continuing series from leading Christian authors and their key messages.

• Based on LifeWay's well-known, interactive model for daily Bible study.

• The interspersed interactive personal learning activities **in bold type** are written by the writer identified on the Study Theme unit page.

• Teaching plans follow each lesson to help facilitators guide learners through lessons.

• Published quarterly.

AMY SUMMERS wrote the personal learning activities and teaching plans this study. Amy, her husband Stephen, and their three children live in Arden, North Carolina. Amy loves teaching and exploring the Word of God with the ladies in her Sunday School class at Trinity of Fairview Baptist Church.

ABOUT THIS STUDY

How much are you willing to risk to become all that God wants you to be?

❑ **Nothing; I don't think it's worth the risk.**
❑ **I'm too scared to risk anything.**
❑ **Some days everything and other days nothing.**
❑ **Everything**

As you study these lessons, ask God to pull you out of your comfort zone and empower you to seize each day for Him.

Fire and Rain:
The Wild-Hearted Faith of Elijah

The greatest heroes of the Bible were also the greatest risktakers for God. That should not surprise us because the life of faith is inherently a life of risk. In the spiritual arena what you risk is what you get. Those who risk little, achieve little. Those who risk the most, gain the most.

These lessons are about a hero whose name you recognize but whose story you may not know. His name is Elijah. He steps onto the stage of biblical history at a low ebb in the history of Israel. When the nation was almost completely given over to idolatry, God raised up a mountain man to confront the evil men who controlled the government of the nation.

I love Elijah because he's a real man. There's nothing fake about him.

With Elijah, you never had to wonder what he was thinking or feeling.

He wore his heart on his sleeve and he captivated a nation.

Are you ready for some excitement?

Are you tired of the status quo?

Are you ready to seize the day?

Join me in this look at the life of Elijah.

Ray Pritchard

Staying Fit ... Spiritually

We talk a lot of the importance of staying physically fit, but what about the health of our spirits? Connect, Grow, Serve, Go is a call to evaluate your present spiritual condition and discover ways to improve your spiritual health. Packed into each biblical concept—Connect, Grow, Serve, Go—is a simple way you can move forward, not remain stagnant. Best of all, these tools will stand the test of time—no "fad" diets here. They will help you become spiritually healthy—and stay that way.

WITH AN OPEN HEART
MARK 12:29-31

IN BODY, MIND, & SPIRIT
ROMANS 12:2

WITH WILLING HANDS
1 PETER 4:10-11

WITH READY FEET
MATTHEW 28:19-20

Connect urges you to worship, pray, fellowship, and relate to others in positive relationships at work, in the home, and in other settings. Spiritual fitness results when you connect with God, with others, and with your church family.

Grow refers to learning and understanding more about God and His expectations of His people, which comes through Bible study. You grow by applying that knowledge to your everyday living.

Serve describes the work you do inside your church. Your church is full of ministry and service opportunities. You serve by using your spiritual gifts, skills, and passions to glorify God. All of us must work together for the church to function as God intended.

Go moves you outside the church and into the community and the world. Evangelism and missions are ways to go into your community and the world in the name of Jesus Christ. It might be uncomfortable at first, but you will experience firsthand the difference Christ can make through you.

Connect, Grow, Serve, Go must impact you before it can permeate your circle of friends, your Bible study group, and then your church as a whole. But balance is the key! We must be actively participating in all four areas if we want to be spiritually healthy. All **Go** and no **Connect** with God or other believers results in powerless activity and wears you out. A steady diet of **Grow** without the action of **Serve** or **Go** leads to unhealthy spiritual obesity and laziness. We need a balanced spiritual diet to remain fit and able to serve God in the ways for which He has gifted us.

The "Leader Guide" after each lesson in *MasterWork* will offer suggestions to help you, your Bible study leader, and your Bible study group to **Connect, Grow, Serve,** or **Go**. Look for these **Connect** ♥, **Grow** 🎧, **Serve** ✋, or **Go** 👣 icons in this and other adult study resources from LifeWay Christian Resources to help you check and maintain your spiritual balance and health.

God's Mountain Man

day One

Seven Evil Kings

This is the story of one of the greatest men of the Old Testament. He was a prophet, and he was a mountain man who came out of nowhere to step onto center stage. He lived by a brook in a ravine and then in a widow's house. He defeated the prophets of Baal on Mount Carmel and then ran and hid in a cave. He was uncouth and unrefined, yet God used him to shake a nation. Because he didn't follow the status quo, he made everyone around him uncomfortable. And we're still talking about him 2,800 years later. His name was Elijah. He was God's mountain man.

In order to understand Elijah, we have to roll back the tape a few generations before he stepped onto the stage of biblical history. Our journey begins in 1 Kings 15. For most of us this is part of the white pages of the Bible. That is to say, it's a section of the Bible we normally don't look at very much unless we're trying to read through the Bible in a year. That's a shame because these chapters contain enormous spiritual truth that we need to learn. The author of 1 Kings traces the story of the kings of Israel and the kings of Judah, and by putting them up against each other, he draws attention to those who walked with God and those who didn't. For our purposes, we will concentrate on the kings of Israel, the name given to the northern 10 tribes after the nation split in 931 B.C. The northern 10 tribes usually are called *Israel*; the southern two tribes usually are called *Judah*. I call your attention to a succession of kings in the northern 10 tribes.

The first king of the northern 10 tribes was a man by the name of Jeroboam.

Read 1 Kings 12:26-33 in your Bible. Would you classify Jeroboam as a good or bad king? Why?

_____

_____

And so Jeroboam introduced idolatry into the nation, and he brought down upon his people the wrath of the Lord God.

Jeroboam was succeeded on the throne by his son Nadab. We pick up the story in 1 Kings 15:25–26: "Nadab the son of Jeroboam began to reign over Israel in the second year of Asa king of Judah, and he reigned over Israel two years. He did what was evil in the sight of the LORD and walked in the way of his father, and in his sin which he made Israel to sin." Nadab reigned for only two years because he was assassinated. "In the third year of Asa king of Judah, Baasha the son of Ahijah began to reign over all Israel at Tirzah, and he reigned twenty-four years. He did what was evil in the sight of the LORD and walked in the way of Jeroboam and in his sin which he made Israel to sin" (1 Kings 15:33–34).

So now we have three kings in Israel, each one worse than the one before:

> Jeroboam
> Nadab
> Baasha

Baasha had a son whose name was Elah. "In the twenty-sixth year of Asa king of Judah, Elah the son of Baasha began to reign over Israel in Tirzah, and he reigned two years" (1 Kings 16:8). Verse 13 mentions that "all the sins of Baasha and the sins of Elah his son, which they sinned and which they made Israel to sin, provoking the LORD God of Israel to anger with their idols." Here's the fourth king, and he's as bad as the first three. After two years a man named Zimri assassinated Elah. First Kings 16:15 says Zimri reigned only seven days. That's hardly long enough to begin the makeover of the palace. You hardly have time to move out the old furniture and move in the new. After one week on the throne, Zimri was assassinated by a man named Omri "because of the sins he had committed, doing evil in the eyes of the LORD, and walking in the ways of Jeroboam

If you desire to dig deeper...

Read the following passages and indicate in the space below the results of Jeroboam's rebellion against God.

1 Kings 13:34
1 Kings 14:1-20
1 Kings 15:27-30
2 Kings 17:18-23

Results:

and the sin he had committed and caused Israel to commit" (1 Kings 16:19, NIV).

So here's the list of kings so far:

Jeroboam

Nadab

Baasha

Elah

Zimri

Omri

Omri was the worst of all. Look at 1 Kings 16:25: "Omri did what was evil in the sight of the LORD, and did more evil than all who were before him."

There is yet one more name in this long list of the evil kings of Israel, a name you will recognize. We are told in 1 Kings 16:28 that "Omri slept with his fathers and was buried in Samaria, and Ahab his son reigned in his place." You've heard that name. These other fellows we don't know much about, but Ahab we know. You've also probably heard of his wife Jezebel.

At last we come to the bottom line.

Read 1 Kings 16:30-33, printed in the margin. Underline the phrases that indicate the degree of Ahab's sin. List what Ahab did to anger God more than any other king of Israel.

So the story unfolds this way:

Jeroboam did evil in the eyes of the Lord.

Nadab his son did evil in the eyes of the Lord.

Nadab was assassinated by Baasha, who did evil in the eyes of the Lord.

Baasha was followed by his son Elah, who did evil in the eyes of the Lord.

Elah was assassinated by Zimri, who did evil in the eyes of the Lord.

Zimri was assassinated by Omri, who did even more evil in the eyes of the Lord.

Omri was succeeded by his son Ahab, who was the worst of all the kings of Israel to this point.

"Ahab the son of Omri did evil in the sight of the LORD, more than all who were before him. And as if it had been a light thing for him to walk in the sins of Jeroboam the son of Nebat, he took for his wife Jezebel the daughter of Ethbaal king of the Sidonians, and went and served Baal and worshiped him. He erected an altar for Baal in the house of Baal, which he built in Samaria. And Ahab made an Asherah. Ahab did more to provoke the LORD, the God of Israel, to anger than all the kings of Israel who were before him" (1 Kings 16:30–33).

From Jeroboam to Nadab to Baasha to Elah to Zimri to Omri to Ahab, we are not going up. The nation is spiraling downward, and it seems that just when you think things can't get any worse, the bottom falls out, and the nation descends even further into idolatry and immorality.

Do you know what Ahab did? According to 1 Kings 16, in the days of Ahab, it became trivial to offer sacrifices to idols.

Ahab was the worst of all, and Jezebel was his evil wife.

What personal challenge did you gain in reading of the downward spiral of the nation of Israel?

_____

day *Two*

And . . . Bam!

That brings me at last to the end of 1 Kings 16 and the beginning of 1 Kings 17. In the *New International Version*, verse 1 begins with the word "now." In the Hebrew it's literally "and." That's important because the author wants us to catch the flow of history from God's point of view. It's "and," not simply "now."

Read in your Bible Romans 5:8; Galatians 4:4-5; and Ephesians 2:3-5. Why are "And Elijah" and "But God" hopeful phrases?

_____

Now we're down in the sewer. The nation is far gone in immorality and idolatry. Things appear to be totally hopeless. But note the little word *and*. Something is about to happen.

God is about to enter the situation.

God's about to interject Himself.

Almighty God is about to be heard.

When times are bad and the situation is hopeless, God has a man. "Now Elijah the Tishbite, from Tishbe in Gilead, said to Ahab" (1 Kings 17:1, NIV). Have you ever watched Emeril Lagasse on the Food Network? If you've seen him, you know what he does when he is preparing a recipe on camera. There's something he says when he's about to add some cinnamon or some salt or some garlic to the mixture. He'll pour it on, and then he'll shout, "Bam!"

A little cinnamon. Bam!

A little salt. Bam!

A little garlic. Bam!

That's what's happening here. "And Elijah . . . said to Ahab." Bam! The prophet of God shows up. No preparation. No warning. No genealogy at all. We don't know anything about Elijah's parents or grandparents. The Hebrews loved genealogy, but nothing is recorded about his background.

Elijah. Bam! Now they've heard from God. When times are bad and the situation is hopeless, God has a man whose name is Elijah. Alexander Whyte called him "a Mount Sinai of a man with a heart like a thunderstorm." F. B. Meyer called him a "colossus among men." Alexander Maclaren called him "the Martin Luther of the Old Testament." Oswald Sanders says, "Elijah appeared at zero hour in Israel's history. . . . Like a meteor, he flashed across the inky blackness of Israel's spiritual night."[1]

Before we go any further, here are a few facts about Elijah:

1. *Elijah was one of the greatest prophets in the Old Testament.* You could easily argue that Moses was the greatest prophet, but he was also a leader of his people. If you want to talk about a pure prophet who wasn't involved in running the government, it's hard to argue against Elijah as the greatest. He comes at the head of the class.

2. *Though Elijah lived almost 3,000 years ago, he speaks to us with amazing contemporary power.* His message speaks to at least five different groups of people.

He speaks to those who have a hard lot in life.

He speaks to those who feel alone in the world.

He speaks to those who feel their life has produced few results.

He speaks to those who feel helpless against the tide of evil.

He speaks to those who have failed, which includes, I suppose, all of us at one time or another.

Which of those categories of people to whom Elijah spoke describes where you are right now in your life? Check it above. Pause to pray, asking God to speak to you through Elijah's life. Ask for the courage to hear God's voice and respond.

3. *We know almost nothing about Elijah's background.* He's a Tishbite, which means he's from Tishbe in Gilead. To this day no one has ever found a village or a town named Tishbe. That simply means it was a small village up in the mountains. Gilead we know, and that's important. Gilead was on the eastern side of the Jordan River. It would be in modern-day Jordan, across the Jordan River from the city of Jericho. In fact, if you ever go to Jericho, look to the east and you will see the mountains of Gilead. That's really the only clue we have about this man.

Elijah was a mountain man. Because he came from the mountains, he was probably a bit uncouth. Because he came from the mountains, he wasn't very refined. Because he came from the mountains, he wouldn't have had the same level of education as those who were raised in the city of Jerusalem. In that day people from the city tended to look down their noses at men from the mountains the same way people today sometimes look down at folks who come from the hills. Hill people. Hillbillies. Elijah was like an Old Testament hillbilly. Before you laugh too much, remember this. You don't want to make those people mad. You'll lose that argument. You might lose something else too. You don't want to mess with mountain folks. They're a tough breed.

day Three

"The Lord Is My God"

Jeroboam
Nadab
Baasha
Elah

Zimri

Omri

Ahab

They're so far down in the pit, a city boy isn't up for that kind of job. God didn't want a seminary graduate. God didn't want anybody too refined. God wanted somebody cut from rough cloth, somebody who didn't mind wearing burlap, somebody with calloused hands, somebody whose nouns and verbs might not always agree. God wanted a man raised in the mountains who was not scared of wicked King Ahab, that evil toad squatting on the throne of Israel. When God wanted a man to go up against that evil king and his evil wife, he had to go to the mountains to find him.

When he did, he got a man. He didn't get a boy. He got a man, and he sent that man to see the king. Elijah's name tells us about his character. *El* is God, and *Jah* is like Jehovah or Yahweh. The *i* in Elijah means "my." Literally Elijah's name means "the Lord is my God." What's your name? "My name is *The Lord is my God*." Any questions?

What is it about you that declares to others *The Lord is my God?* Is it the way you:

- ❑ **Talk**
- ❑ **Work**
- ❑ **Treat others**
- ❑ **Spend money**
- ❑ **Spend your time**
- ❑ **Other**

"Hello, Ahab. Hello, Jezebel. My name is *The Lord is my God*." Ahab was not laughing. He didn't see anything funny about that. You can imagine the color draining out of Ahab's face as this uncouth man from the mountains strides into his presence with a message from the Lord God in heaven. Oh, we need men like that today. Elijah was a troublemaker for the Lord. He was called to serve in a day of moral apostasy.

Read James 5:17 in your Bible. List in the margin other fascinating facts you learned about Elijah.

The *King James Version* says he was a man of "like passions." He was like you, and he was like me. Read the story and see for yourself. Elijah had his ups and downs. He was a little rough around the edges. Not so polished. Not so refined. You're not going to have Elijah over to watch the World Series because you don't know when he's going to go off. He's that kind of man. When he gets a message from God, he's going to take action. You're not going to talk him out of it either. As we will see, he was far from perfect. He's got a temper, and he is prone to depression and discouragement. James used him as an example for us to follow because, despite his human weaknesses, he was a man of prayer who walked with God in the midst of an evil generation. Though he was an imperfect mountain man, he was also a man of prayer and enormous faith in God. And that's why he's in the Bible.

day Four

Elijah's Secret

Consider what Elijah said to Ahab: "As the LORD the God of Israel lives, before whom I stand, there shall be neither dew nor rain these years, except by my word" (1 Kings 17:1). What was Elijah's secret? What made him tick? The answer is right here.

First, Elijah believed in the living God. "Ahab, my God is alive. What about yours? You worship Baal, who lives during the wet season and dies during the dry season. I serve the living God. I believe in the living God."

Read 2 Kings 17:15, printed in the margin. What was the difference between Ahab's Baal and Elijah's God?

_____

_____

"They rejected His statutes and His covenant He had made with their ancestors and the warnings He had given them. They pursued worthless idols and became worthless themselves" (2 Kings 17:15, HCSB).

Second, Elijah served the covenant God. He called him "the God of Israel."

Third, Elijah lived in the presence of God. "The God . . . before whom I stand." Proverbs says the fear of the Lord brings safety. When Elijah stood before Ahab, he was not afraid because Elijah said, "I stand before Almighty God. Ahab, you are nothing to me." One reason we are not bolder and more courageous is because we have more respect for men than we do for Almighty God. The fear of man brings a snare, but he who trusts in the Lord will be kept safe (see Prov. 29:25). So that is no small thing when Elijah says, "I stand in the presence of God." As far as Elijah was concerned, Ahab didn't even matter. All Elijah did was show up and deliver God's message.

> "One reason we are not bolder and more courageous is because we have more respect for men than we do for Almighty God."
> —Ray Pritchard

Read in your Bible Isaiah 51:7-8. Why don't God's people need to fear man?

_____

_____

Fourth, Elijah obeyed the call of God. "There shall be neither dew nor rain these years, except by my word." What does that mean? Ahab worshiped Baal, and Baal was the god of fertility. The Canaanites believed Baal appeared in the thunderclouds and the rainstorms. They set up their altars on mountaintops so they could be closer to their god. When people came to worship Baal, they encountered the men and women who served in the priesthood. There were two parts of the religion of Baal—illicit sex and child sacrifice. If you were praying for rain, you would offer your sacrifice, and then you would have a sexual encounter with a priest or a priestess of Baal. The people believed that somehow the sexual act joined them with Baal, the god of fertility. And if things were really bad, you would bring your children and offer them to Baal. It was a religion of perverted sex and child sacrifice in the name of personal peace and affluence. Does that sound familiar? Nothing in 3,000 years has really changed.

day *Five*

A Radical Man

Elijah's life is the story of a truly radical man. The word *radical* is from the Latin word *radix,* meaning "root." So many of us live in the clouds, and we wonder why we have no courage. Elijah was a man who got down to the root of things.

Read in your Bible Jeremiah 17:7-8. What enables a person to get to the root of things and stay rooted?

_____

You know what a radical Christian is? A radical Christian is nothing more than somebody who's gotten down to the root issues of life and figured out what matters and what doesn't matter. And Elijah had figured it out.

Elijah was a radical man.

We could use a few more like him today.

Here is the question for today: "Where are the Elijahs of the Lord God?"

Read the Bible passages printed in the margin. Then complete the statement below.

The male and female Elijahs of today _____

_____

"Therefore, my dear brothers, stand firm. Let nothing move you. Always give yourselves fully to the work of the Lord, because you know that your labor in the Lord is not in vain" (1 Cor. 15:58, NIV).

"Be on your guard; stand firm in the faith; be men of courage; be strong. Do everything in love" (1 Cor. 16:13-14, NIV).

[1]Cited by Brian Bill, "Running on Empty," Pontiac Bible Church, September 19, 2001.

Before the Session

1. Bring 3 x 5 inch cards for each participant.

During the Session

1. Read: *Those who risk little, achieve little. Those who risk the most, gain the most.* Ask adults if they agree with that statement and to state why or why not. OR Organize the class into groups of two or three. Request adults share with their groups how much of a risk-taker they are on a scale of 1 to 10 (with 1 being not at all). Encourage them to share why they are or why they are not risk-takers. FOR EITHER OPTION Announce that this study of Elijah will challenge participants to be risk-takers so they can become all God wants them to be.

2. Ask why you must know the environment in which a person lives to fully understand the person. Explain that Dr. Pritchard takes readers back several centuries to help them get a feel for the environment in which Elijah ministered. Write "Jeroboam" on a large writing surface, stating that he was the first king of the Northern Kingdom of Israel. Discuss the first activity of Day 1. Request participants describe Jeroboam's reign in two or three words. Write responses next to Jeroboam's name. Use the remarks and Scriptures in Day 1 to list and describe the next five kings. Finally, write Ahab under Omri's name. Complete the final activity of Day 1. Call for descriptions of Ahab's reign. Write responses next to his name. Ask: *Why would it be risky to minister for God in such an environment?* Guide the class to evaluate how the society in which they live resembles Elijah's world. Ask: *Is it still risky to speak for God in our environment? How?* ♥

3. Read the first phrase of 1 Kings 17:1. Explain the term "Now" that begins that phrase is literally "and." Ask how that little word "and" in the midst of this downward spiral of evil kings could inject hope in the situation. State that "But God" is also a hopeful phrase. Invite learners to share how "But God" or "And God" has brought hope to their lives. State that God often sends hope and help by sending His man or woman. God entered Israel's terrible situation through Elijah. Explain the meaning of

To the Leader:

Being a Bible study leader requires a risk! It's risky to try something new in an adult Bible study class to get participants' attention and challenge them to apply what they're studying. Remember, those who risk the most, gain the most.

To get a feel for the man Elijah before you begin to teach these lessons, read his entire story in 1 Kings 17–19,21 and 2 Kings 1–2.

Elijah's name. Determine why that name needs to define anyone who is going to be a risk-taker for God. Challenge adults to silently consider the first activity of Day 3. Use Dr. Pritchard's remarks in Day 2 to describe where Elijah was from. Ask participants what images or words come to mind when they hear the term "mountain man." Consider how that helps them get a better grasp on the kind of man Elijah was. Discuss the final activity in Day 3. Consider the significance of the fact that Elijah had a nature like ours. Ask: *If we live in a world that is similar to Elijah's world, and we have a nature similar to Elijah's nature, then what is our challenge?*

4. Acknowledge that learners may feel completely inadequate to be the kind of risk-taker that Elijah was. State: *That is why believers must learn Elijah's secret.* Invite someone to read aloud 1 Kings 17:1. Request participants identify from Day 4 the first reason Elijah could boldly confront the evil in his day. Discuss the first activity of Day 4. Discuss: *How did the difference in the deities they worshiped make the difference between Ahab and Elijah? What are worthless gods that are worshiped in our day? How do those who pursue those gods become worthless themselves? What is the only way we can be worthy and useful instead of worthless?* Request learners state from Day 4 other reasons that could have been factors in enabling Elijah to have been such a risk-taker for God. Ask why Elijah was not afraid to confront the evil king Ahab. Read aloud Proverbs 29:25. Determine how fearing man snares believers. Discuss the final activity of Day 4.

5. Use the remarks in Day 5 to describe a radical Christian. Ask how we can figure out what matters and what doesn't. Read Dr. Pritchard's closing question. Discuss the final activity of Day 5. Consider how doing "everything in love" requires a radical risk. Distribute 3 x 5 inch cards to participants. Request they write "And (their name)" on the card. Urge them to post that card in a conspicuous place as an encouragement to take risks to speak and act for God. Close in prayer.

Dry Brook University

dayOne

A Sudden Change of Direction

Read 1 Kings 17:1, printed in the margin. Write below that verse what you think would be a good, exciting verse to follow Elijah's pronouncement.

"Now Elijah the Tishbite, from Tishbe in Gilead, said to Ahab, 'As the Lord, the God of Israel lives, whom I serve, there will be neither dew nor rain in the next few years except at my word'" (NIV).

Since Elijah had just come out of the mountains and out of total obscurity, and had been brought by God to stand before the wicked king Ahab, and had declared God's message of coming judgment on the nation, the next verse says what we do not expect, words that must have come as a surprise to Elijah himself. This is what 1 Kings 17:2 says: "And the word of the LORD came to him." I imagine this happened while he was standing before Ahab or just as Elijah was leaving Ahab's presence.

Elijah now receives further instructions from God. "Depart from here" (v. 3). *Here* being the presence of the king. *Here* being the capital of the northern empire. "Depart from here and turn eastward and hide yourself by the brook Cherith, which is east of the Jordan" (v. 3). When you read of the brook, don't think of a river. The word refers to a wadi, a dry creek bed, which during the wet season would be flowing with water but during the dry season would be dry. The prophet receives further instruction in verse 4: "You shall drink from the brook, and I have commanded the ravens to feed you there." So he did what the Lord told him to do. He went to the Cherith ravine east of the Jordan and stayed there.

As I read the story, I ask myself, "Why in the world would the Lord do this?" I think Elijah must have been somewhat disappointed when this word came down from the Lord. It's a bit mystifying if you think about it. First there are those seven evil kings, one after another, dragging the nation into a moral cesspool. Then bam! Elijah steps on the scene. And just as suddenly he disappears. Just as quickly as he comes, just that quickly he is sent into obscurity, silence, and solitude.

"Be still before the LORD and wait patiently for him; do not fret when men succeed in their ways, when they carry out their wicked schemes" (Ps. 37:7, NIV).

"Be still, and know that I am God; I will be exalted among the nations, I will be exalted in the earth" (Ps. 46:10, NIV).

"But the LORD is in his holy temple; let all the earth be silent before him" (Hab. 2:20, NIV).

"Very early in the morning, while it was still dark, Jesus got up, left the house and went off to a solitary place, where he prayed" (Mark 1:35, NIV).

Read the Bible passages printed in the margin. What do you think are reasons God brings silence and solitude into His people's lives? _____

_____

Are you willing for God suddenly to redirect your steps, especially if that redirection leads you in a way you did not plan to go? Are you willing to follow the Lord not just through green pastures by still waters, but are you also willing to follow the Lord if the path leads down to a ravine where you must hide yourself?

day *Two*

Lessons from by the Brook

What lessons should we learn from Elijah's God-directed time by the brook? Let me suggest just a few of them to you.

God's will is revealed to us one step at a time. When God told him to go hide himself in the ravine, what exactly did Elijah know? Elijah knew one thing: He was to go and hide himself in the ravine, and that's all he knew.

Not long ago I heard a man say that when God wants to show us His will, He gives us a flashlight, not a road map. We are given just enough light to peer into the darkness and take the next step. Personally I much prefer to have a road map when I set out on a journey. Better yet, I like having a GPS tracker in my car so that I know where I am at every moment. "Go and hide yourself in the ravine" must have been a disappointing or at least a surprising word. We must learn the lesson that Elijah had to learn, that God's will is revealed to us one step at a time.

If Elijah had any hope of doing all God wanted him to do, his first stop had to be the ravine by the brook Cherith. You can't get around the ravines of life. You can't bypass that part of your spiritual journey. It's a lot more exciting to be up on the mountain facing down the prophets of Baal and calling down fire from heaven. But if you want to get to the mountaintop, you've got to go by way of the ravine. You've got to spend a few years going to school at Dry Brook University.

God's timetable and ours are not the same. Why was it to Elijah's advantage to go and hide himself? For one thing, he had just told the king there would be a drought in the land. But at that moment they had water in their cisterns and food in their storage rooms. It would take quite a few months for the full force of the drought to take effect in the nation. Elijah needed to hide so God could do His work. Second, once the drought began to take hold in Israel, Elijah would be public enemy number one. So hiding Elijah was God's way of protecting him during that time. Third, God wanted to use this drought to expose Baal, who was thought to be the god of fertility. The people believed he was the god who brought the rain that watered their crops. The drought proved that Baal had no real power. The God of Israel is the God of the drought; He is also the God of the rain.

I imagine that life by the creek after the first 150 days or so wasn't really that exciting. But this was God's plan for Elijah. God's timetable and ours are rarely the same. Like Elijah in the ravine, we must be patient and wait for the Divine Conductor to lift His baton and begin the music again.

God's delays teach us to trust Him in new ways. God was doing something in Elijah's life down by the brook Cherith that Elijah didn't fully understand at the time. It's one thing for someone to say God will supply all your needs and He'll take care of you. You've got to come to the place where you decide for yourself whether that's true.

God's power works even in our absence. It is a great advance in the spiritual life when we come to understand that God doesn't need us to do anything. Many of us struggle with this concept. God was doing just fine as God before you showed up. He'll do just fine after you are gone. His power works even in our absence.

> "It is a great advance in the spiritual life when we come to understand that God doesn't need us to do anything."
> —Ray Pritchard

Read Isaiah 55:8-11 in your Bible. What hard truths was Elijah learning in the ravine?

_____

What promise could have encouraged him?

_____

God's blessings come after we obey, not before. The *New International Version* translates verse 5 this way: "So he did what the LORD had told him. He went to the Kerith Ravine, east of the Jordan, and stayed there"

(1 Kings 17:5). What's the most important word in that verse? I'd like to nominate the last word, "there." God's command was tied to a place and to a specific act of obedience. In order to obey God, Elijah had to do some "ravine time." Why? Because *there* is where the brook is. That's where the water is. God is saying, "If you want My blessings, you're going to have to go *there* and stay *there*." Why? Because God's blessings come after our obedience and not before. You're going to have to go there and stay there because that's where God wants you to be.

I put it all together this way:

First there is God's command.

Then there is Elijah's obedience.

Then there is the miracle of the daily feeding by the ravens.

Command, obedience, miracle. We all like the miracle part. We all like the blessing part. We all like answered prayers. We all like the victory. But you will never get to the miracle side unless you go through the command and the obedience first. That's the point. *God's blessings came after Elijah obeyed, not before.*

God's guidance comes through suddenly changing circumstances. Verse 7 tells us that sometime later the brook dried up.

Why did that happen according to James 5:17? (See the text printed in the margin.)

_____

"Elijah was a man just like us. He prayed earnestly that it would not rain, and it did not rain on the land for three and a half years" (Jas. 5:17, NIV).

Elijah had prayed that it would not rain, and the answer to that prayer brought the drought that would eventually lead the nation to repentance. Sometimes we suffer because our prayers have been answered. Your hard times don't necessarily mean you are doing something wrong. They may mean you are doing exactly what God wants you to do. Elijah obeyed God, stayed by the brook; and in answer to his own prayers, the brook eventually dried up. What do you do when the brook dries up? *You pray and you stay and you wait.* F. B. Meyer points out that we all have to stay by a drying brook sooner or later. It may be the drying brook of popularity, or the drying brook of failing health or a sick loved one or a failing career, or the drying brook of a friendship that is slowly fading away. In some ways it is harder to sit by a drying brook than to face the prophets of Baal on Mount Carmel. Why does God allow the brook to dry up? Meyer offered this explanation: "He wants to teach us not to trust in His gifts, but in Himself. He wants to drain us of self, as He drained the apostles by ten days of waiting before Pentecost. He wants to loosen our roots before He removes us to some other sphere of service and education."[1]

What drying brook are you at right now? (Circle those that are appropriate.)

Finances	**Relationships**	**Creativity**	**Energy**
Passion	**Career**	**Other**	

What does God want you to do at that drying brook?

The greatest scenes of Elijah's life are yet to unfold, but God knows exactly what He's doing. There is a universal truth for us if we will receive it. We must all spend some time in the ravine by the drying brook to prepare us for greater work God has for us later.

day Three

Elijah and the Ravens

Let's take a trip into the avian world and think about the ravens that fed Elijah. We begin with a few simple facts. Ravens are large black birds closely related to crows, the main difference being that ravens are bigger, with a wingspan that reaches 50 inches. They can be found from the Arctic to the deserts of North Africa to the islands of the Pacific. During flight they perform complicated aerial acrobatics. Biologists consider them to be extremely intelligent birds. They are capable of a wide range of noises, including the ability to mimic human speech. But that is not their most notable characteristic. *Ravens are scavengers.* They eat berries, fruit, insects, bread, and carrion (the flesh of dead animals). They sometimes kill small birds and mammals such as rabbits and rats. They have even given us a word that describes a person so hungry that he will eat anything. Such a person is said to be ravenous.

Ravens appear in the Bible in only a few places. Genesis 8:6–7 says that when the floodwaters began to recede, Noah sent out a raven in search of dry land. Although the earth was still covered with water, the male raven (one-half of the entire raven population at the time) had no trouble staying alive by scavenging off all the material floating on the surface of the water. In Song of Solomon 5:11, the woman describes her beloved as having hair as "black as a raven." The scavenging side of the raven appears in Proverbs 30:17 where a rebellious child will be thrown in a valley and the ravens will pick out his eyes. Instead of an honorable burial, the rebellious child becomes food for the ravens. Isaiah prophesied that after God judged Edom, it would be so deserted that only the owl and the raven would live there (Isa. 34:11). Despite their negative image, God cares for the ravens, and He feeds them (Ps. 147:9). When Jesus wanted to impress this truth upon His disciples, He told them to "consider the ravens: They do not sow or reap, they have no storeroom or barn; yet God feeds them" (Luke 12:24, NIV).

There is one more fact we need to consider.

Read Leviticus 11:13-15, printed in the margin.
What did God say about the raven in the law He gave to Moses? _____

"These are the birds you are to detest and not eat because they are detestable: the eagle, the vulture, the black vulture, the red kite, any kind of black kite, any kind of raven" (Lev. 11:13-15, NIV).

God doesn't say why the Hebrews were to consider these birds unclean ("detestable") and thus not to be eaten under any circumstances. Ravens may have been included because they eat dead flesh. But this much is certain—*Once God declared the ravens unclean, no Hebrew would have anything to do with them.* And given their scavenging nature, that prohibition was actually a blessing to the Hebrews.

And that brings us back to the story of Elijah. When the Lord told him to go and hide himself by the brook Cherith on the east side of the Jordan, He also promised to send ravens to feed him. I have no doubt that the prophet was not exactly thrilled with that promise. It's hard enough to have to hide yourself in a desolate region. Far worse was the news that he would be fed twice a day by unclean birds. The whole thing was unusual because ravens normally care only for their own. Under no circumstances would they bring food to a man, much less do it twice a day.

What questions might Elijah have had when God said ravens would bring him food?

_____

_____

Read Daniel 4:35, printed in the margin. What truth about God was Elijah learning from his "raven-ous" providers?

_____

_____

"He does as he pleases with the powers of heaven and the peoples of the earth. No one can hold back his hand or say to him: 'What have you done?'" (Dan. 4:35, NIV).

day Four

Lessons from the Ravens

What should we learn from the story of Elijah and the ravens?

1. God commanded and the ravens came. In 1 Kings 17:4 the Lord declares, "I have commanded the ravens to feed you there." I can imagine Elijah sitting alone by the brook when suddenly a flock of birds approaches him. They are ravens, unclean scavenger birds. It must have been a fearsome sight to see these enormous black birds swooping in with bread and meat in their beaks. But they did not come by chance, nor did they fly from a nearby cave. God sent them, God commanded them, God directed them, and thus they came to the prophet's aid.

Let me pause to ask a question. How much food does it take to sustain your family each week? God knows the exact amount because He keeps track of what we need. He knows your name, and He knows your address, and He knows what you need today, and He knows what you will need tomorrow. It's all written on His heart because He watches over you even when you think He has forgotten you. God knows what you need, and He knows when you need it, and He will make sure you have it in time. As He sent the ravens to Elijah, He can command all heaven to come to your aid.

Read Matthew 6:25-34 in your Bible. What truth does Jesus really want you to "get?"

_____

Have you gotten it yet?
❏ **Not at all**   ❏ **I'm getting there**   ❏ **Absolutely**

2. God did not allow Elijah to hoard up a surplus. He sent the ravens to Elijah twice a day, in the morning and again in the evening. The ravens didn't bring enough on Monday to last the whole week. They brought enough in the morning to last the day and enough at night to keep him nourished during the night. Just enough and nothing more. This is what Jesus meant when He taught us to pray, "Give us this day our daily bread" (Matt. 6:11). God is teaching us in the Old Testament the same thing He is trying to teach us in the New Testament. *He is willing to supply our needs but only on a day-to-day basis.* We don't like to live like that. Most of us have freezers at home filled with food. There is nothing wrong with that, but a freezer filled with food makes it difficult to pray this prayer sincerely. We mutter our prayers instead of saying them from the heart because we already know we aren't going to go hungry. We don't want to live day to day. We'd rather have pension plans and stocks and bonds and options. We would rather have life insurance policies that guarantee a secure future. If we had our way, the Lord's Prayer would read, "Give us this week our weekly bread," or, "Give us this month our monthly bread." Or better yet, "Lord, give us this year our yearly bread. Just give it to us all at once and we'll be all right. Then we'll trust You." But that is not how Jesus taught us to pray, and such a prayer would not be good for us anyway. We do better when we are forced to depend on God every day.

Life *is* uncertain. Most of us don't have enough savings to get through more than another month or so. You can be doing fine, and then one day the doctor says, "I'm sorry the tests are positive. You've got cancer." Your life gets rearranged in a split second. Just when you think you've got it all together, an illness, the loss of a job, the collapse of an empire that you put together can happen so fast. God lets those things happen to move us from self-sufficiency to God-sufficiency, from self-reliance to God-reliance, from trusting in our own ability to trusting in Him alone.

Read Luke 12:16-25 in your Bible. Why is it pointless to hoard a surplus?

Why is it pointless to worry?

day *Five*

One Day at a Time

I talked with a single mother who ran her own business. When I asked how things were going, she smiled and said, "We're barely making it. June was tough. But I've got two jobs for July. We're going to be OK for July. That's the way it is. Just when we're about to run out, God brings us a little more work." That's not easy, but she has discovered something that those of us who have plenty of money never discover. She's learning in the laboratory of life that God *will* meet her needs.

Circle the italicized statements that best declare what you REALLY believe God will do about your needs.

And my God   *might / will*   meet   *some of / all*   your needs according to   *what He's able to scrounge up / his glorious riches in Christ Jesus* (Phil. 4:19).

Am I saying that we shouldn't plan ahead? No, I'm not saying that. You should plan ahead. That's biblical. You should plan ahead, but you shouldn't worry ahead. There's a big difference. Here is how Charles Spurgeon brought the truth home:

> Elijah had enough, but it did not always come to him in the nicest way; for I do not imagine that the ravens knew how to get bread and meat always cut into nicest shape. Perhaps they snatched a rough bit of meat here, and perhaps a crust of bread there, and it came in all sorts of ugly pieces, but still, there it was, and it was enough. "Beggars are not to be choosers," we say, and certainly pensioners on God's bounty ought not pick holes and find fault with the Lord's providing. Whatever God gives thee be grateful

for, for if too proud to take from the raven's mouth, it will be well for thee to go without, until hunger consume thy pride. God promises His people enough, but not more than enough, and even that enough may not come to us in the way we should choose.[2]

3. God didn't ask Elijah's permission before He sent the ravens. I'm sure He didn't ask because I think Elijah would have said, "Lord, I've got a better idea." Perhaps Elijah wondered where the ravens got the food they brought him. Did they pick apart some decaying carcass and bring the leftovers to the prophet of God? No, it wasn't like that at all. The same God who commanded the ravens made sure that the food they brought Elijah was good for him. God can take an unclean bird and feed His prophet, and He can do it for days or months or even for years. James 5:17 says that because of Elijah's prayers, it did not rain in Israel for three-and-one-half years. If that's how long he was at Cherith, it means that the ravens served him more than 2,000 meals.

We would have been less surprised if God had used a sparrow or a robin to bring the food. But that is not how God works. He routinely chooses the despised things of the world in order to confound the mighty, and He uses the foolish to bring the strong down to nothing (see 1 Cor. 1:27). As you look at the course of life, you may think that God is going to use some rich uncle or a wealthy friend to help you out. But experience shows how unlikely that is. God is much more likely to meet your needs through the ravens of the earth that fly to your need when you least expect them. The Lord has plenty of ravens to supply the needs of His children. If God sends you to Cherith to hide you for a season, do not despair, for He has not forgotten you. Though you be hidden to man, you are not hidden to your Heavenly Father. He knows where you are, and He knows why you are there. Do not be surprised when a flock of large black birds gathers to your hiding place. They are God's ravens, sent from heaven to bring you food.

4. God has appointed the beginning and ending of every season of life. First Kings 17:7 says "some time later the brook dried up" (NIV). That makes it sound as if it happened by chance. But the Hebrew phrase translated "some time later" actually means "at the end of days." It means the brook dried at the end of the days appointed by God. The water ran as long as God decreed, and on the day He decreed, the brook began to dry up.

Read Ecclesiastes 3:1-11 in your Bible. What can you say with certainty about every season in your life?

_____

The same God who sent the rain also sent the drought. The same God who called Elijah to confront Ahab also sent him to hide by the brook. The same God who sent the ravens now sends him to live with the widow of Zarephath. As the narrative of Elijah's life unfolds, it appears to take many wild swings.

From the mountains of Gilead,

To the king's palace,

To the brook Cherith,

To a widow's home in Zarephath.

But what seems to be haphazard and unplanned is actually the unfolding of God's divine plan. When God determines to do something, it will happen. You can write it down and take it to the bank.

Elijah moves on to his next assignment from the Lord.

He doesn't see any of this in advance. It's always on a "need to know" basis.

Would you like to be like Elijah? If we are willing to obey, God will take care of the details. He can send the ravens to feed us when the world has forgotten us. Meanwhile enjoy the brook and be grateful for the ravens.

Read Psalm 78:19-20, printed in the margin. How would Elijah have answered the Israelites' cynical question?

_____

How has God spread a table in the desert for you?

_____

"They spoke against God, saying 'Can God spread a table in the desert? When he struck the rock, water gushed out and streams flowed abundantly. But can he also give us food? Can he supply meat for his people?'" (Ps. 78:19-20, NIV).

[1] F. B. Meyer, *Elijah and the Secret of His Power, www.bibleteacher.org* (accessed July 28, 2006).

[2] Sermon by C. H. Spurgeon, "God's Care of Elijah," *Metropolitan Tabernacle Pulpit,* vol. 57, 510–11, Ages Software.

leader Guide

Sometimes Sunday School classes go through dry brook times. People quit coming, discussions seem dull, and leaders wonder if they are making any difference. When you go through those dry brook times as a leader of adult Bible study, don't give up in discouragement. Thank God for this valuable training time. Pray for wisdom and endurance to stay at that dry brook until God has done all He wants to do with you there.

Before the Session

1. Obtain a flashlight, roadmap, and GPS tracker (if possible).
2. Obtain an enlarged copy of a few bars of musical notes; make sure a musical rest notation is included.

During the Session

1. Ask: *What university would you have attended if money, grades, or location had not been a factor? Why?* OR Organize the class into teams. Request each team answer: *Where would you recommend people go for training if they wanted to: 1. Become an engineer; 2. Develop strict physical discipline; 3. Hone their musical skills; 4. Become a faithful servant of God.* FOR EITHER OPTION Remark that we might not be too interested in attending Dry Brook University, but that is exactly where God sent Elijah to prepare him for the ministry that lay ahead.

2. Call for responses to the first activity of Day 1 [Example: "And lo, thunder crashed and the ground shook. Ahab rent his robes and fell to his knees before Elijah in repentance."] Request someone read aloud 1 Kings 17:2-4. Ask if participants think it's odd that Elijah began his public ministry, spoke one sentence, and then left for the desert. Request that learners explain their responses. Invite volunteers to read aloud Mark 1:9-12 and Galatians 1:15-18. Lead the class to determine how Jesus' and Paul's experiences were similar to Elijah's. Consider why obscurity, silence, or solitude is a difficult but necessary university for God's children to attend. [The second activity of Day 1 can help with that discussion.]

3. Point out that Day 2 details lessons Elijah learned at DBU (Dry Brook University). Display a flashlight, map, and GPS tracker. Ask which item represents how God reveals His will. Ask someone to read aloud the first italicized lesson in Day 2. State that God does not overwhelm His children with more of His will than they can bear to know. He gives them just enough light to know what they need to know for the next step. Request someone read aloud the second italicized lesson statement. Lead the class to consider reasons it was to Elijah's advantage to

hide at the brook for several months. Invite participants to describe what they think was a typical day for Elijah at the brook. Ask: *What do we do during the dry, monotonous times of life?* Ask someone to read aloud the next two italicized lesson statements. Read aloud the quotation in the margin. Allow learners time to reflect on why that is both a humbling and relieving truth. Discuss the Isaiah 55 activity. Inquire: *How have you learned the same truths and been encouraged by the same promise? Why would Isaiah 55:18-19 be a good motto for Dry Brook University?*

4. Invite a volunteer to read aloud 1 Kings 17:5-6. Discuss how Elijah learned the lesson that God's blessings come after we obey, not before. Read aloud 1 Kings 17:7. Consider what Elijah might have been thinking when the brook dried up. Read aloud the following statement: "Your hard times don't necessarily mean you are doing something wrong. They may mean you are doing exactly what God wants you to do." Display the musical bars and point out the rest notation. Ask the following questions, allowing time to discuss each: *How are the rests in music just as important as the notes? How are the rests in our lives just as important as times of action? What are some rests or "dry brook times" in adults' lives? Do we usually choose them or are they forced on us? Why does God allow dry brook times? What must we do with our dry brook rest times?*

5. Ask participants what comes to mind when they think of a raven. Ask: *Under what circumstances would you eat food that had been in a raven's beak?* Use Day 3 to explain how ravens were regarded by the Jews. Discuss the final activity of Day 3. State that God had more lessons for Elijah to learn at DBU and He used the ravens to teach those lessons. Encourage participants to state lessons they would have learned from the ravens if they had been Elijah.

6. Discuss the two activities in Day 4. Consider the difference between responsibly saving (planning ahead) and hoarding (worrying ahead). Lead the class to evaluate how God's children can live one day at a time in an economic system of monthly paychecks and bills.

7. Complete the final activity of Day 5. Allow volunteers to share the most valuable lesson they have learned from Dry Brook University.

8. Close in prayer.

Empty Barrel Graduate School

day One

Four Tests for Elijah

Before Elijah was ready to go face the prophets of Baal, there was one more stop he must make. God had some testing in store for his servant. "Then the word of the LORD came to him: 'Go at once to Zarephath of Sidon and stay there. I have commanded a widow in that place to supply you with food'" (1 Kings 17:8–9, NIV). Before Elijah would be ready for the big challenge on Mount Carmel, there were four tests he must pass.

1. The Test of a New Place—Zarephath was a small village in Sidon, in the region of modern-day Lebanon. It was north of the land of Israel. The geography matters because there is someone else in this story who came from Sidon. Her name was Jezebel, Ahab's pagan wife. Sidon was a center of Baal worship. And now God was taking His servant from the brook Cherith and sending him to Zarephath in Sidon. To get there Elijah had to travel into Gentile territory, into the region of Baal worship; and when he got there, he was somehow to meet a widow who would tell him what to do next. Verse 10 tells us Elijah's response: "So Elijah got up and went to Zarephath. When he arrived at the city gate, there was a widow woman gathering wood" (HCSB). Note a couple of things. The word *Zarephath* comes from the Hebrew word for smelting place, meaning it once housed a furnace where they produced iron by heating the ore until the iron separated from the dross. The iron would then be used for the construction of weapons and chariots. Elijah was being sent from the brook into the furnace, so to speak.

Consider how difficult this must have been. He was to go and meet a woman. In that culture that was not easy to do. He was to go and meet a Gentile woman. For a Hebrew man that was doubly difficult. He was to go and meet a Gentile woman who was a widow. This meant that when he found her, she was going to be very poor.

And notice one other thing. God told Elijah to go to Zarephath and "stay there." First Elijah was to stay by the brook. Then he was to stay in a widow's house in Zarephath. That's not an easy command for a man of action like Elijah. Elijah had been by himself for a long time, hiding by the brook. The brook had dried up, and God had sent him into Baal's backyard. His orders were simple: Stay there.

As you read the translations of Hebrews 10:36 printed in the margin, underline the various terms that describe staying-power. Why does God tell His children to "stay there"?

_____

You can imagine Elijah thinking something like this: *Lord, I have been here long enough, and now You are sending me into Gentile territory to find a widow who is dirt poor, and You want me to stay there. I am called to preach the Word, and I am called to bring the nation back to You. Lord, what are You doing?* It can be humbling, and it can be frustrating when God says, "Stay where you are."

"Lord, I want to go someplace else."

"Stay there."

"Lord, I don't like this job."

"Stay there."

"Lord, I don't really like my neighbors."

"Stay there."

"Lord, I'm not too happy in my marriage."

"Stay there."

"Lord, I'm tired of my church."

"Stay there."

The first test was the test of a new place. Not just are you willing to go there, Elijah, but are you willing to go and stay there?

2. The Test of First Impressions—"'Go at once to Zarephath of Sidon and stay there. I have commanded a widow in that place to supply you with food.' So he went to Zarephath. When he came to the town gate,

"For you have need of endurance, so that when you have done the will of God, you may receive what was promised" (NASB).

"But you need to stick it out, staying with God's plan so you'll be there for the promised completion" (The Message).

"You need to persevere so that when you have done the will of God, you will receive what he has promised" (NIV).

"For ye have need of patience, that, after ye have done the will of God, ye might receive the promise" (KJV).

a widow was there gathering sticks" (vv. 9–10, NIV). That's about as hope-less a situation as you could find. A widow dressed in a widow's garb gath-ering sticks. Elijah doesn't offer to help her. Instead he asks her to help him. "He called to her and asked, 'Would you bring me a little water in a jar so I may have a drink?' As she was going to get it, he called, 'And bring me, please, a piece of bread'" (vv. 10–11, NIV). This may seem heartless, but it is the only way the prophet can know for sure if she is the widow God intended him to meet. Her response reveals that she is the right one: "'As surely as the LORD your God lives,' she replied, 'I don't have any bread—only a handful of flour in a jar and a little oil in a jug. I am gather-ing a few sticks to take home and make a meal for myself and my son, that we may eat it—and die'" (v. 12, NIV). Things aren't looking hopeful for the prophet of God. When he gets to Zarephath, he meets a widow who is gathering sticks to cook one final meal after which she and her son will starve to death.

You think, *If I change my circumstances, things are going to get better.* Don't count on it. Change isn't bad. Sometimes we need to make a change. But change doesn't always improve your outward circumstances.

Here is the test we all have to face. *Am I willing to obey God even when it doesn't make a whole lot of sense?* When you are called by God to speak to the nation, it doesn't make sense to go spend a long time hiding by the brook, and it makes even less sense to go to Zarephath and meet some widow who is down to her last meal. That's not what you would call upward career mobility. But it's in the Bible. There's a whole lot of life that doesn't make sense. It's not a bad thing; it's a test from God because if God made it easy, we'd take Him for granted. If God made it easy, we wouldn't pray so much. If God made it easy, we'd think better of ourselves than we should.

Elijah had to go to Zarephath, the smelting place. He had to spend some time in a desperate situation. Why? It was good for him. He needed it. He needed to stay with a widow because she taught him compassion. There was no other way for him to learn it.

3. The Test of a Hopeless Situation—This poor widow is gathering sticks to prepare a final meal before she and her son die together. If ever there was an impossible situation, here it is. Elijah said to her, "Don't be afraid." I'm sure she was glad to hear that. Then he gave her some strange instructions.

Read Elijah's instructions in 1 Kings 17:13-14 in your Bible. In the space below, record anything Elijah said that may not have made sense to the widow.

From a human point of view, this makes no sense whatsoever. By every standard of reasonable calculation, this poor widow and her son will soon starve to death. All the evidence pointed in that direction. Elijah had only two things to go on at this point. *First, he had the memory of what God had done in the past. Second, he had God's Word in the present.* He remembered how God had taken care of him by the brook, and he knew that God had called him, and so he knew that somehow God would take care of him, and God would take care of that widow and her son.

How have God's provisions in the past given you confidence for whatever "empty jar and jug" situation you're facing right now?

It must have been hard for him to say those words. It must have been hard for her to hear those words. But somehow she had faith to believe what Elijah said.

4. *The Test of Obedient Faith*—The Bible says in verse 15 that "she went away and did as Elijah told her" (NIV). Literally the Hebrew says, "She went and did." Here is the end of the story: "So there was food every day for Elijah and for the woman and her family. For the jar of flour was not used up and the jug of oil did not run dry, in keeping with the word of the LORD spoken by Elijah" (vv. 15–16, NIV). This was a pure miracle from God. When the barrel is full of oil, you don't need faith because you've got all the oil you need. Faith comes in when you are almost out and you don't know how you're going to go to fill it up again. That's when you find out how much faith you have.

Personally I much prefer when the barrel is full of oil. You don't have to worry so much. You don't have to think about where the next meal is coming from. It's good when the barrel is full of oil. It's not so good when the barrel of oil is nearly empty. But in the kingdom of God, the values of life are completely reversed, which is why this story speaks to modern Christians, especially to Western Christians who live in such prosperity compared to the rest of the world. *For the people of God, abundance is generally much more dangerous than lack.* That's why Jesus said it is hard for a rich man to enter the kingdom of heaven (Matt. 19:23)—not because money is bad, but when you have money, you depend on it. And that is why the poor often respond quickly to the gospel and those who have a lot often don't feel their need for God because their barrel is full. Although I prefer to live with a full barrel, God often lets the barrel run out because it's better for me to live in want than in abundance.

day *Two*

God Often Multiplies Tests

Elijah's journey demonstrates that God often multiplies His tests. We finish one test and bam! Here comes another one. God does it to keep us humble. He does it to purify us. He does it because we need it even though we don't like it very much. First He sends us to Dry Brook University; and as soon as we are finished there, He enrolls us in Empty Barrel Graduate School. Why? *God sends the tests to make us stronger.* Once we are stronger, we are ready to take the next step. Nothing in Elijah's life happens by chance. Every step has been ordered by the Lord to prepare him for greater work to come. From the mountains to the palace to the brook and now to the widow's home in Zarephath. God was preparing his man every step along the way. God does the same thing for you and me.

Read Proverbs 16:1-9 in your Bible. What do you learn about the steps you take in life?

Through the long months by the brook and in Zarephath, God was building character into Elijah's life that could be reproduced in other people. Let's pause to consider what Elijah learned at Cherith and Zarephath:

At Cherith Elijah learned, "God can take care of me."

At Zarephath he learned, "God can use me to take care of others."

Elijah needed the brook, and he needed the widow's house because they taught him lessons he couldn't learn any other way. That leads me to make a simple application.

When God says go, don't analyze it. Just go.

When God says stay, don't analyze it. Just stay.

We've all got to do some "ravine time" and some "furnace time." It's part of God's preparation to make you what He wants you to be so that like Elijah, when the moment comes, you'll be ready to take the next step with Him.

What Zarephath furnace are you at right now?

_____

Read 1 Peter 1:7, printed in the margin. What is God's desired end to your furnace time?

_____

"These have come so that your faith—of greater worth than gold, which perishes even though refined by fire—may be proved genuine and may result in praise, glory and honor when Jesus Christ is revealed" (1 Pet. 1:7, NIV).

day Three

A Mother's Sorrow

That brings us to the story of the death of the widow's son in 1 Kings 17:17–24. The story begins this way: "Some time later the son of the woman who owned the house became ill. He grew worse and worse, and finally he stopped breathing. She said to Elijah, 'What do you have against

"Moses returned to the LORD and said, "O Lord, why have you brought trouble upon this people? Is this why you sent me?" (Ex. 5:22, NIV).

"And Joshua said, 'Ah, Sovereign LORD, why did you ever bring this people across the Jordan to deliver us into the hands of the Amorites to destroy us? If only we had been content to stay on the other side of the Jordan!'" (Josh. 7:7, NIV).

"'But sir,' Gideon replied, 'if the LORD is with us, why has all this happened to us?'" (Judg. 6:13, NIV).

"What is man that you make so much of him, that you give him so much attention, that you examine him every morning and test him every moment? Will you never look away from me, or let me alone even for an instant? If I have sinned, what have I done to you, O watcher of men? Why have you made me your target? Have I become a burden to you?" (Job 7:17-20, NIV).

me, man of God? Did you come to remind me of my sin and kill my son?'" (1 Kings 17:17–18, NIV).

There are so many mysteries about why God does what He does. I'm reminded of the words of Tony Evans, who said, "Everything in the universe is either caused by God or allowed by God, and there is no third category." That's a hugely important statement. So many times we look at heartbreaking tragedy, and we want to invent a third category called, "Bad things that just happened for no reason." But there is no such category. When the text says that it came about that the child grew ill, it's the writer's way of saying that what happened to this young boy was not an accident. It was not chance. It was not fate. God was present in the home when that boy died.

The timing of all this deserves our attention. The boy got sick after many weeks and months of miraculous provision by God. After many months of the flour and the oil never running out, suddenly the boy got sick and died. Why does it happen that way? We walk with the Lord and we do the best we can, and one day the phone call comes that changes life forever. Or we get a report from the doctor with bad news. Or our children get into terrible trouble. Or our marriage falls apart. Why do these things happen?

As you read the Bible passages printed in the margins of pages 38-39, check the ones that reflect the "why" questions you've asked God.

It is very easy for us to become complacent in the midst of the blessings of God. We secretly begin to think: *Everything's OK now; I've got life all wired up. My marriage is good, and my kids are good, and my job is good, and life is good, and I love my church. Everything in my life is exactly where I want it to be.* If that happens to be your situation at this moment, don't feel bad about that. If your life is like that, you ought to enjoy it, and you ought to be profoundly grateful to God. But know these two things for certain:

1. You don't deserve these blessings.
2. They won't last forever.

They never do. Soon enough the clouds will move in, and the rain begins to fall. You shouldn't live in fear, but you ought to be wise enough to know that after sunrise comes sundown, and after high noon comes the darkness of midnight. So it is for all of us sooner or later.

Read in your Bible Matthew 5:45. Who gets rain in their lives?

_____

Now read Job 2:10 in your Bible. What is a realistic attitude about the rain in our lives?

_____

After the time of God's blessing, disaster strikes. We don't know why the child got sick. It almost seems like a contradiction. There was the testing, then the blessing, and then the sorrow. It seems like it ought to be reversed, turned around somehow, like it ought to be sorrow and then testing and then blessing. But that's not how God works. It's more often this way: Testing—Blessing—Sorrow.

Of all the sorrows of life, I know of no sorrow greater than the death of a child. Nothing seems more unnatural. Parents are not supposed to bury their children. It is the privilege and the honor of children to bury their parents. It is not supposed to be the other way around.

I don't know why the widow's son died. The mother's dreams were dashed. She didn't see this coming at all. If you go back and read the text, she thought she and her son would die together because of the famine in the land. Now in her anguish and sorrow, she blamed Elijah. "What do you have against me, man of God? Did you come to remind me of my sin and kill my son?" (1 Kings 17:18, NIV).

There are at least three problems with her thinking. *First, she seems to have thought that having a prophet in the house made her immune from suffering.* Who could blame her, especially after all the miraculous provision of the flour and the oil? But she was wrong. *Second, she assumed that her own sin somehow caused her son's death.* But that does not appear to be correct in this instance. *Third, she blamed Elijah.* It's human to find someone to blame when tragedy strikes.

"Why, O LORD, do you stand far off? Why do you hide yourself in times of trouble?" (Ps. 10:1, NIV).

"My God, my God, why have you forsaken me? Why are you so far from saving me, so far from the words of my groaning?" (Ps. 22:1, NIV).

"I say to God my Rock, 'Why have you forgotten me? Why must I go about mourning, oppressed by the enemy?'" (Ps. 42:9, NIV).

39

Read Romans 8:31-39 in your Bible. How can you know for certain whether or not you get any answers to your "why" questions of life?

The Prophet's Faith

I find Elijah's response instructive when the mother accuses him of coming to her house just to kill her son.

1. He doesn't get angry.
2. He doesn't try to explain why her son died.
3. He doesn't argue with her.
4. He doesn't make any excuses.

Instead he responds with incredible gentleness.

Read Galatians 5:22-23, printed in the margin. How is it evident to you that Elijah was filled with the Spirit of God?

"But the fruit of the Spirit is love, joy, peace, patience, kindness, goodness, faithfulness, gentleness and self-control" (Gal. 5:22-23, NIV).

When the widow made her unkind accusation, Elijah responded simply. All he said is, "Give me your son" (v. 19a). When I go to visit a family where a death has occurred, I don't say as much as I used to. In my earlier years I would often do lots of talking. Looking back, I think I felt nervous and awkward, and I think I felt a need to try to explain things. I don't say much anymore. For one thing, I find that people in sorrow don't remember much that you say anyway, and there is always a danger of saying too much.

"He took him from her arms, carried him to the upper room where he was staying, and laid him on his bed. Then he cried out to the LORD, 'O LORD my God, have you brought tragedy also upon this widow I am staying with, by causing her son to die?' Then he stretched himself out on the boy three times and cried to the LORD, 'O LORD my God, let this boy's life return to him!'" (1 Kings 17:19a–21, NIV).

There is no easy way to explain what happens next. Elijah lies down on top of the body of the child. Foot to foot. Leg to leg. Chest to chest. Arm to arm. Hand to hand. Face to face. He does it not once, not twice, but three times. No one really knows exactly why he lay down even once, much less why he did it twice or three times. Perhaps Elijah understood that to do anything for this boy he was going to have to get personally involved. As a side note, since the boy was dead, he was now unclean under Hebrew law. It was wrong for a prophet of God to touch a dead body, but extreme cases call for extreme measures. And so by lying down on the body of the child, it is as if he were saying, "Oh Lord, take some of the life from within me and give it to this boy." Elijah prayed for a miracle because he believed in a power greater than death.

A. W. Pink pointed out seven noteworthy features of Elijah's prayer:

1. He went to his private room where he could be alone with God.
2. He prayed fervently.
3. He relied on his personal experience, calling him "My God."
4. He recalled God's sovereignty in causing this child to die.
5. He prayed earnestly and persistently.
6. He appealed to God's tender mercy toward this poor widow.
7. He made a definite request: "Let this boy's life return to him."[1]

Where did Elijah learn to pray like that? Where is the precedent in the Bible prior to Elijah for anybody praying that way? Before this moment no one had ever been brought back from the dead. This is the first case in biblical history of anyone who died and came back to life.

When Elijah prayed, he submitted himself completely to God. In himself the prophet had no power to bring this child back to life. He doesn't demand anything from the Lord, nor does he "name it and claim it." He humbly asks God to "let this boy's life return to him." That was as much as he could do. The rest was up to God.

Read 2 Corinthians 12:7-9 in your Bible. How did Paul demonstrate the same fervency and submission as Elijah?

How did God's response to Paul's prayer differ from His response to Elijah's prayer?

_____

How did God reveal His power and love to both Paul and to Elijah?

_____

day *Five*

Resurrection Hospital

Now we see how God responds to Elijah's prayer. "The LORD heard Elijah's cry" (v. 22). I love that. The text does not say the Lord heard Elijah's prayer, though he prayed. It says, "The LORD heard Elijah's cry."

When the Bible says, "The LORD heard Elijah's cry" (1 Kings 17:22), it means that when Elijah stretched himself out on that boy's dead body, something happened. God spoke from heaven and said, "All right, man of God, it shall be done." The boy's life returned to him and he lived. That boy who was dead came back to life. It's a pure miracle of God.

We come now to the end of this amazing story. Seeing that her son has come back to life, the grateful mother declares to Elijah, "Now I know that you are a man of God and that the word of the LORD from your mouth is the truth" (1 Kings 17:24). The Bible doesn't record that she said, "Thank you," though surely she did. It's not recorded here because that's not the point. *Her words explain the miracle, and they also explain why not every mother receives this miracle when a child is sick to the point of death.* The miracle happened to authenticate Elijah as God's anointed prophet. God had promised to sustain all three of them—mother, son, and Elijah—until the rains came and the drought ended (v. 14). On the basis of that promise, Elijah believed that God would bring the boy back to life. Strange as it may sound, the miracle is less about the boy and more about God's power working through Elijah. It is a miracle of sovereign grace, given this one time in Elijah's life and never again given during his ministry. God answered *this* prayer by *this* man in *this* way at *this* particular moment in time. And He did it for His own purposes. There is no other way to understand the story.

"Now I know," she says. Compare that with verse 18 where she speaks bitterly to Elijah. Her bitterness turns to faith as she comes to understand that God only wounds in order to heal. When the child is raised to life, the widow is encouraged, and the prophet is affirmed.

Read the Scriptures printed in the margin. What does God promise to do? _____
How are we to respond? _____

"See now that I myself am He! There is no god besides me. I put to death and I bring to life. I have wounded and I will heal" (Deut. 32:39, NIV).

"For he wounds, but he also binds up; he injures, but his hands also heal" (Job 5:18, NIV).

In our journey through Elijah's life, we have come to the end of the period of his personal preparation. Little does he know that he will soon confront the prophets of Baal in the greatest public showdown of his life.

Let's review Elijah's preparation. Think of it this way:

He lived in the ravine when he attended Dry Brook University.

Then he moved on to Empty Barrel Graduate School.

Now he has finished an internship at Resurrection Hospital.

No one becomes a man of God by chance, and no one becomes a man of God overnight. All these things were part of Elijah's training to make him ready for the work God had for him to do.

What did Elijah learn from these three episodes?

At the brook he learned, "God can take care of me."

From the empty barrel he learned, "God can use me to help others."

From the child that died he learned, "God can work through me to do the impossible."

God's preparation is finished. Elijah is now ready for the ultimate challenge.

"Come, let us return to the LORD. He has torn us to pieces but he will heal us; he has injured us but he will bind up our wounds. After two days he will revive us; on the third day he will restore us, that we may live in his presence" (Hos. 6:1-2, NIV).

[1]A. W. Pink, *The Life of Elijah*, [online] n.d. [cited 28 July 2006] Available from the Internet: *www.pbministries.org/books/pink/Life_of_Elijah/elijah_10.htm.*

Briefly describe in the margin episodes in your life when you learned:
"God can take care of me."
"God can use me to help others."
"God can work through me to do the impossible."

leader Guide

During the Session

1. Ask: *What is the purpose of testing?* OR Invite participants to state what they thought were the best and worst parts of high school or college. FOR EITHER OPTION Remind learners that last week the class explored lessons Elijah learned at Dry Brook University. Sometimes a lesson is best learned through the test. Today participants will examine some tests Elijah had to pass before he moved on to the next level of ministry.

2. Invite someone to read aloud 1 Kings 17:7-9. Use Dr. Pritchard's remarks to explain why the location of Zarephath in Sidon was a test for Elijah. Ask: *Why would the command to "stay there" be a difficult test? In what "furnaces" might God tell us to stay? What does it take to stay there?* [Use the first activity in Day 1 to help with the discussion.] Ask a volunteer to read aloud 1 Kings 17:10-12. Point out that Dr. Pritchard called this the test of first impressions. Consider what Elijah's first impression of the widow would have been. Evaluate why it would have been a refining experience for the mountain man Elijah to ask a widow to provide for him. Ask: *Whom might we dismiss as being of little or no use to us? When have you discovered that your first impressions were completely wrong?* Ask how the widow's response to Elijah would have given him the first impression that he had gone from a bad to an even worse situation. Invite participants to share how they thought a change was going to make things better and instead their situation worsened. Ask what test we must face in those situations. Explore why God calls us to obey Him even when His commands don't make a lot of sense. Discuss the second activity of Day 1. Debate: *Was this a test for the widow or Elijah? Why might God have chosen this Gentile widow to participate in Elijah's ministry training?* Invite responses to the third activity of Day 1. Inquire: *When might we start complaining about just having flour and oil? How can we keep sight of the miracle?* Consider why abundance is more dangerous than need. Ask: *How can we pass the test of a full barrel of oil?*

3. Invite participants to recall their general frame of mind during final exam weeks. Agree it is very stressful to have one test follow right after another. Remark that God multiplied Elijah's tests. Explore why God sends one test after another when we'd really like to have a break. Ask: *What might we think about God when we go straight from the dry brook into the hot furnace?* Ask someone to read aloud Hebrews 12:5-10. Determine what we can really know about God when He multiplies our tests. 🖤

4. Invite someone to read aloud 1 Kings 17:17. Request volunteers read aloud the Scriptures printed in the margin of Day 3. Ask which "why" questions participants think Elijah and the widow might have asked. Invite learners to voice "why God" questions they have had. Guide the class to consider some possible answers for those "why" questions. Use Dr. Pritchard's remarks in Day 3 to add to the discussion. Affirm that "I don't know" is a satisfactory answer to all those questions. Discuss the last activity in Day 3. State that in her grief the widow was understandably not to the point of grasping God's unshakable love. Read aloud 1 Kings 17:18. State and discuss the three problems with the widow's thinking.

5. Brainstorm possible ways Elijah could have responded to the widow's accusations. Read aloud 1 Kings 17:19-23. Discuss the first activity of Day 4. Point out the seven features of Elijah's prayer. Ask: *Do all fervent, humble prayers get answered the way Elijah's did?* Discuss the last activity of Day 4. ✋

6. Request someone read aloud 1 Kings 17:24. Determine why God answered "Yes" to Elijah's prayer. State that this may have been the first biblical instance of someone being brought back from the dead but it's not the last. Have the class (or small groups) examine the following Scriptures and determine how each instance is similar to and different from the episode in 1 Kings 17:17-24: Mark 5:35-43; Luke 7:11-17; John 11:33-45; Acts 9:36-42. [Point out that the compassion displayed and the end result of God receiving glory is similar in all the instances.]

7. From Day 5 highlight the lessons Elijah learned from the three episodes. Invite responses to the final activity. Close in prayer.

Obadiah: A Good Man in a Hard Place

day One

Elijah's Disappearing Act

Read 1 Kings 18:1-15 in your Bible.

Who was completely in control of the situation? ____

Who was desperate for control? _____

Ahab was angry, and that wasn't good news.

It wasn't just that he was having a bad day or a bad week or even a bad month. For Ahab things had gone bad for the last three years. That's a long stretch of bad luck, and it was bound to make a man grouchy, nervous, tense, upset, uptight, irritable, frustrated, and prone to losing his temper. You didn't want to be around the king when he was in a bad mood, which was most of the time.

Thoughtful observers of the court could pinpoint the exact moment when things began to go south. It happened the day that a strange man named Elijah came to the king's court in Samaria. The man they called a prophet of the living God had declared that there would be no more rain or dew in Israel. It wasn't a long speech. In fact, no one could remember anyone ever making a shorter speech to the king. And it wasn't as if Elijah had been scared. If anything, he seemed almost eerily calm, as if he weren't afraid of anything the king could do to him. This strange man from the mountains of Gilead had walked in, delivered his one-sentence message, and then he suddenly disappeared.

It was the disappearing part that got to Ahab. That plus the drought and the famine. After Elijah vanished into thin air (or so it seemed), he evidently took the rain with him because just like that, the weather report for Samaria was always the same: clear skies, plenty of sun, no clouds, and no rain. Thus it had been for over three years.

The first few months had not been hard because you could always find some food and a bit of water if you knew where to look. But as the days passed, the storehouses emptied, the streams dried up, and a man with a bucket of water possessed a commodity more precious than gold. Soon the reports filtered in of crops that would not grow, of fields turning brown, of ground turned hard, of donkeys collapsing and cows that gave no milk. Slowly the poor began to starve to death. The king had to do something.

But what?

No wonder he was angry and upset. He was the most powerful man in Israel (or so he thought), and yet he was helpless to stop the drought. No matter how many prayers he offered to Baal, the heavens were shut up, and the rain would not come. To make matters much worse, Elijah had disappeared. Vanished with the wind. No one knew where he was, no one had seen him since that fateful day when he spoke his one-sentence message from God.

Read 1 Kings 18:12 and 2 Kings 2:16, printed in the margin. What did some people think was the cause of Elijah's sudden appearances and disappearances?

"I don't know where the Spirit of the Lord may carry you when I leave you" (1 Kings 18:12, NIV).

"Perhaps the Spirit of the Lord has picked him up and set him down on some mountain or in some valley" (2 Kings 2:16, NIV).

Where had he gone?

The king had stopped at nothing to answer that question. That's why he sent soldiers on a manhunt to the surrounding nations. In his frenzied paranoia to capture Elijah, he not only searched in other countries but he also made their leaders swear they didn't know where the prophet was. But try as he might, he couldn't find the mountain man who brought drought and famine to his land.

Now at last the word of the Lord came to Elijah again. "Go and present yourself to Ahab, and I will send rain on the land" (1 Kings 18:1, NIV). It must have come as a relief to Elijah to know that the time had come to confront the wicked king once again. Elijah was preeminently a man of action, and I do not doubt that many nights he must have wondered why he was languishing by the brook and in the widow's home while a tide of wickedness swept over his homeland. Surely he must have prayed and asked the Lord to do something. Perhaps he dreamed up various plans and strategies, but whatever he thought and however he prayed, it is entirely to Elijah's credit that he did nothing until God gave him the green light.

"Wait for the LORD; be strong, and let your heart take courage; wait for the LORD!" Ps. 27:14, ESV).

**Read Psalm 27:14, printed in the margin.
Do you think it takes more strength and courage to act or wait? Explain briefly.**

day *Two*

Elijah, Meet Obadiah

But it was not Ahab that Elijah met. As Elijah journeyed from Zarepath to Samaria, Elijah met Obadiah, who was in charge of Ahab's palace. In modern terms we would say he was Ahab's chief of staff, his right-hand man, the one who kept everything running smoothly. He took care of all the details so that Ahab could busy himself being king of Israel. If you stop to think about it, Obadiah must have been a man of considerable talent because this was a position with enormous responsibility. Obadiah was in charge of everything that happened in the palace. He had oversight of all the servants, the waiters, the helpers, and all the people who came in and out to see the king. *This certainly meant that Ahab must have known Obadiah well and placed a great deal of trust in him.* Get the wrong person in such a position, and your reign might be short. Find the right person, and your life suddenly becomes a lot easier. We all understand that there is the man who sits on the throne, and there is the man behind the throne who makes it all happen. The man on the throne gets the publicity, but it's the unseen man who deserves the credit. That was Obadiah.

Precisely at this point the story becomes fascinating because the Bible tells us two different and seemingly contradictory facts: (1) Ahab was a wicked man who did more evil than all the kings that preceded him. (2) Obadiah was a godly man who feared the Lord from his youth.

How did it come to pass that a godly man should be in charge of the palace for such a wicked man? We do not know the answer because the Bible tells us nothing about Obadiah's family background.

Read the following verses in your Bible and state what we know about Obadiah:

1 Kings 18:3

1 Kings 18:4

1 Kings 18:12

Obadiah somehow managed to serve the Lord and to keep his high position even while serving a king bent on leading the people into a spiritual free fall.

Elijah never could have served in Ahab's court. Never! Such a thought would have been abhorrent to him. Why would he, a prophet of God, serve in the court of a man given to such wickedness? But that was evidently exactly where God had placed Obadiah.

Elijah was a mountain man, not suited to the refined life of a king's court.

Obadiah had the training and temperament to serve the king well. He would not have survived long in the mountains of Gilead.

If Elijah didn't understand Obadiah, and if Obadiah feared Elijah, it is perfectly understandable.

But the prophet needed Obadiah whether he knew it or not. For it was Obadiah who paved the way for the prophet to meet the king again.

Read John 21:20-22 in your Bible. How would you summarize Christ's response when His servants tried to question one another's roles or futures?

Baal Buster

Carmel is an enormous mountain by the seacoast overlooking the modern-day city of Haifa. From the top of Mount Carmel you have a commanding view in all directions. Carmel was important in the Old Testament for military and geopolitical reasons. Whoever held Mount Carmel controlled the northern half of the nation. And whoever controlled the worship that took place on Carmel controlled the nation spiritually. The priests and the prophets of Baal knew that. That is why years earlier they had built an altar to Baal on top of Mount Carmel.

Baal worship was a bizarre mixture of idolatry, perverted sexuality, and child sacrifice. The pagans believed Baal controlled the rising and the setting of the sun. He was also considered the god who brought forth the seasons, the god who brought forth or withheld the rains. Because ancient Israel was an agricultural nation, Baal was an extremely powerful deity. Men and women who came to worship Baal would offer a sacrifice and then engage in some sort of sexual activity with the priests and priestesses. They believed that if you were joined physically to one of those priests or priestesses of Baal, the power of Baal would be transferred to you. Thus Baal worship appealed on one level to the mind, on another level to their economic well-being, and on a deeper level to the desires of the flesh.

We should therefore not be surprised that Baal worship became extremely popular. It grabbed the mind, the heart, the body, and ultimately the soul. Under the reign of wicked king Ahab, Baal worship had virtually swept the Northern Kingdom. The worship of the one true God had been almost completely extinguished.

God tapped Elijah on the shoulder and said, "Go see Ahab again." When the king and the prophet met the second time, the king asked, "Is that you, you troubler of Israel?" (1 Kings 18:17, NIV). The Hebrew word for *troubler* sometimes means "snake." "You dirty snake." That's what the king thought of God's anointed prophet. Elijah turned the tables and said, "I have not made trouble for Israel. . . . But you and your father's family have. You have abandoned the LORD's commands and have followed the

Baals" (v. 18, NIV). Before Ahab could say anything else, Elijah said, "It's time for the truth to come out. It's time for the people to decide." He said to the king, "Tell all the people of Israel to meet me at Carmel." That was agreeable to the king. Elijah said, "Send 450 prophets of Baal, and send 400 priests of Asherah." That's 850 false prophets versus one man of God.

Asherah was a leading female deity in the Canaanite religion, considered to be the wife of El, the chief god. Commonly regarded as the goddess of fertility, she was worshiped at groves of evergreen trees or places marked by wooden poles. The Bible repeatedly warns against the worship of Asherah (Ex. 34:13; Deut. 7:5; Judg. 6:25; 2 Kings 23:4).

On the appointed day they met on top of Mount Carmel. We pick up the story in 1 Kings 18:20–21. "So Ahab sent word throughout all Israel and assembled the prophets on Mount Carmel. Elijah went before the people and said, 'How long will you waver between two opinions? If the LORD is God, follow him; but if Baal is god, follow him'" (NIV). The most important part comes in the next sentence. "But the people said nothing."

Has your response to a challenge to your faith been: vastly different OR disappointingly similar to the people's response? (Circle one.)

Of all the things that plague modern Christianity, perhaps this is the greatest. Spiritual indecision. Spiritual juggling. The inability of the people of God to make up our minds, to decide which side we're really on.

Read the following passages in your Bible and note what choice you must make.

Deuteronomy 30:19-20: I must choose between

_____ or _____

Joshua 24:15: I must choose between serving

_____ or _____

Psalm 119:29-30: I must choose between

_____ or _____

John 3:36: I must choose to either

_____ or _____

Hebrews 11:24-25: I must choose to either

_____ or _____

Note the little word *if.* The word *if* means you have to make up your mind. There is a time to think, and there is a time to decide. *If* the Lord is God. Is He or isn't He? Here is one of the reasons I love Elijah. *He made it practical and personal.* He did not say, "If the Lord is God, buy a book and think about it." He said, "If the Lord is God, get on His team and follow Him. And if Baal is god, fine, then get on his team and follow him. But stop sitting on the fence. You've got to decide sooner or later."

850 to 1

Elijah proposed a simple experiment so the people would know which God was the true God.

> **Read 1 Kings 18:22-24 in your Bible. What test did Elijah propose to determine whether Baal or the Lord was the true God?** _____

We could use more of that sort of courage today. We need a little less talk and a lot more action. There comes a time when talk is cheap. The people of Israel were halting between two opinions. "We think maybe our God is God. Or maybe Baal is God. Maybe we can mix the two somehow." A little of this, a little of that. Elijah said, "No, now the time has come to make up your mind."

The story itself is simple. The prophets of Baal cut up a bull and laid the pieces on the wood, but Elijah would not let them set it on fire. "Ask Baal to light the fire for you." He told the prophets of Baal and Asherah to do whatever they thought they needed to do in order to entice Baal to send fire from heaven. Don't imagine some sedate prayer meeting. Think of wild screaming and various sexualized antics up on the mountain. They carried on for hours, calling out, "O Baal, answer us. Answer us." Nothing happened. At noon Elijah began to taunt them. "Shout louder! . . . Surely he is a god! Perhaps he is deep in thought, or busy, or traveling. Maybe he is sleeping and must be awakened" (v. 27, NIV). Elijah is definitely not politically correct. We don't do this sort of thing anymore. We don't make fun of other people's religion. You get in trouble for doing that. If you did what Elijah did, you might be arrested for a hate crime.

When Elijah suggests that perhaps Baal is busy, he uses a Hebrew word that has a variety of meanings. Some say that the word means that he's gone off hunting. Others suggest it means to go to the bathroom. That's quite an insult if you think about it. Elijah is a mountain man. He's not afraid of embarrassing people.

Toward the end of the afternoon, in desperation the prophets of Baal took knives and swords and began cutting themselves as a kind of blood sacrifice to their false god. How desperate they were.

Read 1 Kings 18:28-29 in your Bible. Describe the response to their desperate prayers.

_____

The heavens were silent. Baal had utterly failed.

day *Five*

The Soaking Wet Sacrifice

First Kings 18:30 is perhaps the most important verse in the chapter: "Then Elijah said to all the people, 'Come here to me.' They came to him, and he repaired the altar of the LORD, which was in ruins" (NIV). Taking 12 stones, one for each of the 12 tribes, he rebuilt the altar of the Lord. *This was a symbolic sign that the nation would now return to its true spiritual heritage.* The timing is also significant. Elijah rebuilt the altar late in the afternoon, about the time of the evening sacrifice. This was the time God had appointed, but Israel had completely forgotten about it. Now at the appointed hour for the evening sacrifice, Elijah built the altar, dug a trench, and laid the wood in place. He cut up the bull, laid the pieces on the wood, and then told the people to soak the wood with four large jugs of water. Three times he ordered the water poured. Until that bull was soaking wet. Until the wood was soaking wet. Until the altar was soaking wet. Until there was so much water it filled the trench around the altar.

By doing these radical things at the time of the evening sacrifice, Elijah was saying, "Our God is a covenant God. If we come back to Him according to His word, He will not turn us away. If we come back to Him on His terms, in the right way at the right time, He will come through for us." Though the people had forgotten, God still was ready to keep His promise.

So at the hour of sacrifice, everything was ready. But they needed a miracle. So Elijah stepped forward and prayed a simple prayer: "O LORD, God of Abraham, Isaac and Israel, let it be known today that you are God in Israel and that I am your servant and have done all these things at your command. Answer me, O LORD, answer me, so these people will know that you, O LORD, are God, and that you are turning their hearts back again" (vv. 36–37, NIV).

On one side you have 850 prophets of Baal and Asherah; and you have eight, nine, ten hours of screaming and yelling and whooping and cutting themselves; and you have all their prayers to their fake God. You have all that religiosity. And over here you have one man, the mountain man, God's man.

Reread 1 Kings 18:36-37. Elijah prayed God would answer him so the people would know:

1. That God was _____

2. That Elijah was _____

3. That God was turning _____

Elijah's only concern was for God, His word, His work, His glory, and His people. Lord, answer me. No screaming. No whooping. No hollering. No cutting himself. I am impressed by the simple dignity of it all.

And when God answered, He answered completely so there could never be any doubt. The fire consumed the sacrifice. The fire consumed the wood beneath the sacrifice. The fire consumed the water in the trench. The fire consumed the rocks of the altar.

As the story comes to an end, three things happen:

First, the people finally wake up, their eyes are opened, they fall down and cry out, "The LORD, he is God; the LORD, he is God."

Second, the people seize the prophets of Baal. Elijah had them brought to the Kishon Valley where they were slaughtered. The prophets of Baal were a spiritually malignant tumor inside the body of the people of God. Elijah wasn't going to leave any part of that tumor inside the body of the nation of Israel.

Third, it started to rain.

Read 1 Kings 18:41-46 in your Bible and 1 Kings 8:35-36, printed in the margin. What do you think Elijah was doing as he bent down to the ground?

_____

"When the heavens are shut up and there is no rain because your people have sinned against you, and when they pray toward this place and confess your name and turn from their sin because you have afflicted them, then hear from heaven and forgive the sin of your servants, your people Israel. Teach them the right way to live, and send rain on the land you gave your people for an inheritance" (1 Kings 8:35-36, NIV).

Seven times Elijah sent his servant to look toward the sea. Six times the servant saw nothing, but the seventh time he saw a cloud about the size of a man's hand. When the rain started, Ahab retreated to his summer palace in Jezreel. Here is the final verse of this story: "The power of the LORD came upon Elijah and, tucking his cloak into his belt, he ran ahead of Ahab all the way" (v. 46, NIV).

Let me challenge you with the words of Elijah put in a contemporary context: _If Jesus Christ be God, follow Him! If anything else or anyone else be God, follow him!_ But make up your mind. Stop playing games. Stop your spiritual juggling. Stop working both sides of the street. Stop sitting on the fence. Take your stand for what you know to be true.

Read Joel 3:14, printed in the margin. What valley of decision are you in right now? _____

What is your decision? _____

"Multitudes, multitudes in the valley of decision! For the day of the LORD is near in the valley of decision" (Joel 3:14, NIV).

To the Leader:

This lesson on making the choice to let God have control is an excellent opportunity to urge people to make the choice to accept Christ as their Lord and Savior. Be prepared to make that evangelistic appeal. Use the evangelism article on the inside cover page if necessary.

During the Session

1. Invite participants to describe situations where they have asked (or at least wanted to ask), "Hey, who's in control here?" OR Write "work, home, school, sports team" on a writing surface. Organize the class into two teams. Instruct one team to list evidences that seem to demonstrate that no one is in control in the situations listed on the writing surface. Instruct the other team to list evidences that demonstrate someone is in control in those situations. Invite groups to share and discuss their lists.

2. Ask a volunteer to read aloud 1 Kings 18:1-2. Consider how it would have seemed that nobody was in control in the land of Israel. Point out that the Israelites, led by King Ahab and his wife Jezebel, were worshiping Baal, whom they believed to be in control of the weather. Ask: *What do you think the Israelites had been asking Baal for the past three years? What do you think they were believing by now about Baal's control of nature? How did the drought prove God was completely in control?* State that the famine had accomplished God's purpose of making the people doubt Baal's power. He'd also used that time to prepare Elijah for the coming showdown between Baal and Jehovah.

3. Point out that God had been working in another servant's life as well. Invite someone to read aloud 1 Kings 18:3-6. Ask: *What did Ahab think he was sending Obadiah to do?* Point out the irony of Ahab not wanting to kill his animals when he'd sanctioned the slaughter of the Lord's prophets. Ask someone to read aloud 1 Kings 18:7-16. Ask: *Why did Ahab really send Obadiah in that particular direction?* Point out that God had plans for Obadiah. Use the first activity in Day 2 for insight into Obadiah. Allow adults to debate whether it was wrong for Obadiah to work for such a wicked man as Ahab. Ask: *Who had the harder job— Obadiah or Elijah? Who had the more important job—Obadiah or Elijah? How did both Obadiah and Elijah demonstrate God was in control of them?* Point out that God has placed us where He wants us; no position is more or less important. What's important is that we allow God to be in control in whatever positions we serve. 🎧

NOTES

4. Ask someone to read aloud 1 Kings 18:16-20. Lead the class to determine how Ahab tried to take control of the situation. Ask: *Why did Ahab think Elijah was the one troubling Israel? How did Elijah reverse the charges? Why do you think Ahab complied with Elijah's request?* Point out that Ahab was ready for a showdown. Use Dr. Pritchard's remarks in Day 3 to explain why Elijah chose Mount Carmel for the showdown and asked for prophets of Baal and Asherah. Ask: *What would you say would be workable odds if you had to have a showdown against opponents—one on one, three against one?* Lead the class to consider how Elijah's three years at the brook and with the widow prepared him to courageously take on the odds of 850 to 1.

5. Read aloud 1 Kings 18:21. Brainstorm how contemporary adults are faced with that challenge daily. Complete the last activity of Day 3. Inquire: *How are all these choices actually your choosing who's going to be in control of your life?* Ask how the people responded to Elijah's call for a decision. Consider how we make a decision when we say or do nothing. 🔘

6. Ask someone to read aloud 1 Kings 18:22-24. Ask how the people were going to determine whether Baal or God was in control. Read aloud 1 Kings 18:25-29. Encourage participants to state words that describe the prophets of Baal and their efforts to get Baal to respond. Complete the final activity of Day 4. Inquire: *What do you think those prophets were feeling in the morning? at noontime? by the evening?*

7. Request a volunteer read aloud 1 Kings 18:30-39. Contrast Elijah and his actions with the prophets of Baal. Ask: *Why do you think the prophets were so out of control and Elijah was so in control?* Ask someone to read aloud 1 Kings 18:40-46. Consider how God proved once again that He was completely in control. Invite someone to read aloud Isaiah 46:1-10. Ask what God wants His people to understand. Help learners determine why it is best for us that God is in control. Point out that we do have the control of choice. Read aloud the final paragraph of Day 5. Urge participants to prayerfully complete the final activity. Learners do not have to verbally share their written responses, but allow time for a couple of members to bring the decisions and those making them before the Lord in prayer. 🔘

Prophet on the Run

day One

The Thrill of Victory,
the Agony of Defeat

When last we visited our hero, he had won his great victory over Ahab and the prophets of Baal at Mount Carmel. *Immediately the story moves from his greatest victory to his most humiliating defeat.* Without a pause we go from the top to the bottom. This is the story of Elijah's battle with discouragement, despondency, and depression.

I'll remind you of what had just happened. Elijah had been up on the mountain where he faced down the 850 prophets of Baal. It was 850 to 1. The prophets of Baal danced around and moaned and groaned and cut themselves, but nothing happened. Then Elijah prayed a simple prayer asking God to demonstrate His mighty power that the hearts of the people might be turned back to the Lord. Immediately fire from heaven came down, consuming not only the offering on the altar but also licking up all the water that was in the trench. The people of Israel bowed down and said, "The LORD, he is God; the LORD, he is God." All the prophets of Baal were slaughtered. An enormous thunderstorm came in from the ocean, drenching the land and breaking the drought. The story ended with Ahab heading back to Jezreel to bring the bad news to Jezebel. But Elijah was so pumped up that he outran Ahab's chariot.

You would think that the next chapter might begin this way: *"And Elijah rejoiced in the Lord his God. He made a sacrifice to give thanks to God, and all the people came to Elijah, and he preached unto them the word of the Lord."* But that's not what happened. Elijah ended up a long way away from Jezreel. He headed south down to Beersheba. He headed south and west far out of the land of promise back down to Mount Horeb, which is another name for Mount Sinai. Hundreds of miles away, he holed up in a cave and prayed for God to take his life.

What do you think caused Elijah to reach such a low point?

_____

We all understand that depression is a major problem in our time. Every year in America 9.5 percent of all adults are diagnosed with some degree of clinical depression. Experts tell us that one out of every four women will suffer from clinical depression at some point and one out of every ten men. Researchers attribute that difference in numbers to the fact that men are far less likely to admit their problems and far less likely to seek help. Depression costs American companies $44 billion a year. It is the leading cause of disability in America. We know that there are many causes for depression, and these things are often interrelated, including stress, difficulty in personal relationships, medical problems, poor diet, trauma, and genetic factors. Symptoms include persistent sadness, feelings of hopelessness, loss of energy, difficulty concentrating, sleeplessness, and irritability, and sometimes it may lead to thoughts of suicide. Researchers tell us that depression seems to be spread across all sectors of society. No one is exempt, and it's not a matter of IQ, age, or social class. Some of the greatest people in history have struggled with feelings of depression.

Read Psalm 42 in your Bible. Record phrases that indicate the psalmist was depressed.

_____

What appears to have been the cause of his depression?

_____

What did he do to positively work his way through the depression?

_____

day Two

Elijah's Condition Examined

You can just imagine with what eagerness Jezebel, that evil shrew, waited for the return of her husband Ahab. When she saw his chariot returning from Mount Carmel, she assumed it must be with good news. When he came into the palace at Jezreel, I am sure his face was ashen.

No doubt she asked him what happened on the mountain. Since it was raining across the land, I suppose Jezebel took it as a sign that the prophets of Baal had won the day. Ahab gave her the bad news.

"What happened to the prophets of Baal?"

"They're all dead."

"What happened on top of the mountain?"

"The Lord God of Elijah won the day, and Baal was defeated."

Jezebel was going to get even. She sent a messenger to Elijah with some ominous news: "May the gods deal with me, be it ever so severely, if by this time tomorrow I do not make your life like that of one of them" (1 Kings 19:2, NIV). I think it's the *tomorrow* part that got to Elijah. He was not a man who would have been easily flustered by a nonspecific threat. Jezebel is saying, "Check your watch, man of God, because by this time tomorrow, I'm going to slice you and dice you the same way you did the prophets of Baal."

Read 1 Kings 19:1-4 in your Bible. What most surprises you about Elijah's response to Jezebel's threat?

_____

How did Elijah respond? *First, he was gripped by fear and doubt* (v. 3). But why should Elijah have been afraid of this woman? He just saw God do a miracle. And he helped slaughter her false prophets.

Second, he reacted impulsively. The text says that he ran from Jezreel, which is in the northern part of Israel, not far from the Sea of Galilee, all the way to Beersheba, the far southern border of the nation. He ran south past Jerusalem, past Bethlehem, past Hebron. Elijah was so scared that he decided to run as far from Jezebel as he could get. That meant a change in climate because Jezreel is pastureland, but in Beersheba he was in the desert.

Third, he wanted to be alone. "When he came to Beersheba in Judah, he left his servant there" (v. 3, NIV). That was a big mistake. The one thing he most needed was somebody to encourage him. Leaving his servant in Beersheba, he ventured into the desert a day's journey, sat under a broom tree, and prayed that he might die. Elijah was on his way to the most remote place he could find. When you're gripped by fear and doubt, you want to run away and be by yourself.

Fourth, he allowed himself to be controlled by dark thoughts. Ever felt this way? "Lord, I've had enough. Lord, this is it. Take my life. I am a total failure." At this moment mighty Elijah, God's mountain man, was filled with self-pity. Having temporarily lost his focus on God and being gripped by fear and doubt, he ran away from his problems. Overwhelmed by despair, he was filled with dark thoughts. This can happen to any of us.

Read 2 Corinthians 1:8 and 7:5, printed in the margin. Does reading about Elijah's and the apostle Paul's dark emotional state disturb or comfort you? Why?

'We do not want you to be uninformed, brothers, about the hardships we suffered in the province of Asia. We were under great pressure, far beyond our ability to endure, so that we despaired even of life" (2 Cor. 1:8, NIV).

"For when we came into Macedonia, this body of ours had no rest, but we were harassed at every turn—conflicts on the outside, fears within" (2 Cor. 7:5, NIV).

day Three

Elijah's Condition Diagnosed

If you study the biblical record, it seems clear that three things have happened to Elijah to bring him to this breaking point. These three things are understandable, they go together, and they can happen to any of us at any time.

First, he was overstrained mentally. It is possible to be under so much pressure for such a long period of time that the spring of life is wound so tightly and eventually it must break. Consider Elijah's career as a prophet. From the mountains of Gilead to the king's palace to the brook to the widow's home to the showdown on Mount Carmel, it's been one crisis after another. The late Tom Landry, coach of the Dallas Cowboys, was fond of saying, "Fatigue makes cowards of us all." Everyone has a limit. You've got your limit, and I've got mine. It's a good thing to realize when you've come to the end, and it's a good thing to realize before you get to the end.

Second, he was exhausted physically.

Read Mark 6:31 in your Bible. What did Jesus tell His disciples to do?
❑ **Get out there and work harder.**
❑ **Spend more time in prayer and Bible study.**
❑ **Come apart and rest for a while.**

Vance Havner was fond of saying, "If we do not come apart and rest awhile, we will simply come apart." There is a time when you need to get up and go to work, and there is a time when you need to lie down and take a nap. Sometimes the best thing we can do for the Lord is to take a vacation. Play tennis. Ride your bike. Watch a football game. Knit a sweater. Have a date with your sweetheart. Play with your grandchildren. Eat an ice cream cone. Take an evening, make some popcorn, sit on the couch, and watch a video.

Third, Elijah was out of touch spiritually. "Elijah was afraid and ran for his life" (1 Kings 19:3, NIV). The Hebrew text contains a phrase that disappears in some modern translations. The first phrase of verse 3 literally reads, "And when he saw." That's his fundamental problem. His mind is overstressed. His body is physically exhausted. And now his eyes are off the Lord and they're on his circumstances. That's what happens when you are under enormous mental stress, when you are physically exhausted, when you've been running on Red Bull and four hours of sleep a night, and you've been burning the candle at both ends.

No wonder Elijah gets scared. He's been under enormous pressure for so long that he can't think clearly. Give him three nights of good sleep, and Jezebel won't bother him so much. When you have been under stress for a long time, you don't think clearly, and you make bad decisions that get you in trouble. That's why the little phrase in verse 3 is so important: "And when he saw." When he was on the mountain, all he could see was God. The prophets of Baal didn't bother him at all. The circumstances didn't matter. It was Elijah and God. But now in his state of emotional exhaustion, he sees Jezebel, he hears Jezebel, and where normally he would have stood his ground, he turns pale, runs for cover, keeps on running, and doesn't stop till he ends up in a cave on Mount Sinai hundreds of miles away.

The mighty prophet of God cowers in a cave, wishing to die, feeling utterly alone, lost in his own despair. But God is not through with his servant yet. Though he ran as fast and as far as he could, Elijah could not outrun the Lord. God has much more work for him to do so Elijah can't stay in the cave forever. Though he made many mistakes, he is still God's man.

In Day 2 you read of Paul's "dark cave time" in 2 Corinthians 1:8 and 7:5. Read those verses once again along with the verses printed in the margin. Answer the following:

1. Why might God allow those dark cave times?

_____

_____

2. What can we be certain God will do when we are depressed?

_____

_____

day **Four**

How to Help a Caveman, Part 1

Elijah was in trouble. He was messed up, depressed, discouraged, stressed out, burned out, mentally fried, physically drained, and spiritually out of sorts. *In other words, he's exactly like many of us.*

"We do not want you to be uninformed, brothers, about the hardships we suffered in the province of Asia. We were under great pressure, far beyond our ability to endure, so that we despaired even of life. Indeed, in our hearts we felt the sentence of death. But this happened that we might not rely on ourselves but on God, who raises the dead. He has delivered us from such a deadly peril, and he will deliver us. On him we have set our hope that he will continue to deliver us" (2 Cor. 1:8-10, NIV).

"For when we came into Macedonia, this body of ours had no rest, but we were harassed at every turn—conflicts on the outside, fears within. But God, who comforts the downcast, comforted us" (2 Cor. 7:5-6, NIV).

First Kings 19 not only tells us what happened to Elijah; it also describes how God met him at his lowest point. Elijah needed four things, and those four things he received from the Lord.

1. Elijah needed rest and refreshment. Elijah sat under the broom tree so discouraged that he prayed that he might die. Then he fell asleep. The Lord sent an angel with a command from heaven: "All at once an angel touched him and said, 'Get up and eat'" (1 Kings 19:5, NIV). How's that for spiritual advice? Get up and eat. He doesn't say, "Get up and pray." He doesn't say, "Get up and read the Bible." He doesn't say, "Get up and start preaching." He doesn't say, "Get up and serve the Lord." The angel tells Elijah to get something to eat.

Here's a profound truth. *Sometimes we need to eat.* Sometimes we need to sleep. Sometimes we need to eat and sleep even more than we need to pray. Sometimes the most spiritual thing you can do is to get up and have a good meal because you'll feel so much better.

So the angel gave Elijah a specific command: "Get up and eat" (NIV). Elijah looked around and found a cake of bread baked over hot coals and a jar of water. He ate and drank, and then he lay down and slept again. God's mountain man is tuckered out. He took a nap. He got up, had some food, and went back to bed again. Is he a sluggard? No. He's just worn out in the service of God. "The angel of the LORD came back a second time and touched him and said, 'Get up and eat, for the journey is too much for you'" (v. 7, NIV). Strengthened by that food, he traveled 40 days and 40 nights until he reached Horeb, the mountain of God. There he went into a cave and spent the night.

Why did Elijah go to Horeb? Because he knew Mount Sinai was the place you went when you know you need to meet God. He didn't pick just any mountain. If he wanted to find a cave, there were caves a lot closer than Horeb. He went back to where Moses met the Lord. There is a value in going back to certain places. There's a value in going back to certain milestones in your life and certain physical locations in your life, places where you met God in the past.

When you are depressed, you need three things, and God made sure Elijah got all three of them.

You need good food.

You need some rest.

"The LORD is close to the brokenhearted and saves those who are crushed in spirit" (Ps. 34:18, NIV).

You need some physical exercise. I would consider walking 40 days across the desert good physical exercise.

Read Psalm 103:13-14, printed in the margin.
God recognizes your physical frame is frail dust.
Do you?   No   Yes
God has compassion on you. Do you have compassion on yourself?   No   Yes
Indicate one way you will give yourself a break today.

"As a father has compassion on his children, so the LORD has compassion on those who fear him; for he knows how we are formed, he remembers that we are dust" (Ps. 103:13-14, NIV).

God's restoration of Elijah begins with rest and relaxation for the body, the mind, and the soul. But there is more to come.

2. Elijah had to face his fears. "And the word of the LORD came to him. 'What are you doing here, Elijah?'" (v. 9, NIV). That's a good question. The last time we saw Elijah, he was winning a great victory on Mount Carmel. So what is he doing cowering in a cave, hundreds of miles away? This question was not for God's benefit but for Elijah's.

Read Elijah's response in 1 Kings 19:9-10. What tone
of voice do you think he used?
❑ **Whiny self-pity**
❑ **Storming anger**
❑ **Mumbling sullenness**
❑ **Frantic panic**

Everything he said was true. He had been zealous. The people had rejected the covenant. They put the prophets to death. No exaggeration at all. If he had stopped there, he would have been on solid ground. Now look at the next sentence. "I am the only one left, and now they are trying to kill me too" (v. 10, NIV). The last part of that sentence is true; the first part was not true. But it was that first part, that feeling of being utterly alone, that needed an adjustment. Elijah was so far gone in self-pity that he actually thought he was the only righteous man left in Israel.

Let me make a simple application. *Self-pity is the enemy of all spiritual growth.* As long as you feel sorry for yourself, you'll make a thousand excuses for not facing your own problems, and you'll never get better.

day *Five*

How to Help a Caveman, Part 2

As God continued to deal with His discouraged servant, He provided two more things that Elijah needed.

3. Elijah needed a new vision of God. Rest and relaxation speak to the body; facing his fears and his self-pity speaks to his mind; a new vision of God speaks to the need of his soul. Elijah needed to be changed body, mind, and soul.

When Elijah began to wallow in self-pity, notice how God responded. God did not condemn him. It doesn't help us when we're depressed if somebody condemns us, and it doesn't help for us to condemn somebody else. It just makes the situation worse.

What follows is amazing. Read 1 Kings 19:11-13 in your Bible and complete the following:

God did not speak to Elijah in the _____ nor in the _____ or the _____ but with a _____ _____.

Why do you think that is significant?

_____

Why does God put Elijah through this demonstration of divine power? *He's getting His man back in touch with spiritual reality.* Psalm 46:10 says, "Be still, and know that I am God." The Lord wants Elijah to know that it is not in the earthquakes or the fire or the huge events where we most often encounter the Lord. We more often meet God in the small, forgotten places of life.

Read Isaiah 30:15, printed in the margin. Why aren't we always willing to find our salvation and strength in rest and quietness?

_____

"For thus the Lord GOD, the Holy One of Israel, has said, 'In repentance and rest you will be saved, in quietness and trust is your strength.' But you were not willing" (Isa. 30:15, NASB).

Our problem is we want to see the earthquake; we want to see the fire all the time. We want the big demonstration. We want the spectacular answer to prayer. God says, "That's not always where you're going to see Me, but just listen for the gentle whisper." God always speaks loud enough for the willing ear to hear.

4. Elijah needed a new commission. In verse 13 God repeats His question, and Elijah repeats his answer. There are times when a mistake must be corrected with accurate information. So now God is going to give Elijah some accurate information. The Lord said to him, "Go back the way you came, and go to the Desert of Damascus" (v. 15, NIV). That's a long journey from the Sinai desert, through the Holy Land, all the way up to the desert around Damascus. Then God had some specific instructions: "When you get there, anoint Hazael king over Aram. Also, anoint Jehu son of Nimshi king over Israel, and anoint Elisha son of Shaphat from Abel Meholah to succeed you as prophet. Jehu will put to death any who escape the sword of Hazael, and Elisha will put to death any who escape the sword of Jehu. Yet I reserve seven thousand in Israel—all whose knees have not bowed down to Baal and all whose mouths have not kissed him" (vv. 15–18, NIV).

God reminded Elijah that he wasn't not alone. Not only was God with him, but God had another 7,000 in Israel who had not bowed down to Baal.

Learn this lesson: *You are not in a position to estimate your own effectiveness.* When you think you've won, don't be so sure. When you think you've failed, let God render the final verdict. You and I are as likely as Elijah to estimate wrongly both our victories and our defeats. Better to do our best and leave the results with God. He knows better than we do the lives that have been changed by our service for Christ.

What is God whispering to you right now?

_____

To the Leader:

Without a doubt there are adults in your class who are struggling or have struggled with depression. Analyze how God dealt with Elijah's depression and consider how you can apply those same acts of gentle graciousness to those in your class who may have this condition. Pray that this will be a liberating, not condemning, lesson for every class participant. But remember, neither you nor your class are professional counselors or psychologists, so your goal should be to express Christian grace and love, not diagnose conditions or prescribe remedies.

During the Session

1. Invite participants who have climbed a mountain to describe what they felt on the mountaintop. Ask: *What's inevitable when you're on the mountaintop?* Agree that at some point you've got to come down. OR Encourage adults to consider what the following men have in common: Abraham Lincoln, Charles Spurgeon, Mozart, Michelangelo, Martin Luther, Winston Churchill, Buzz Aldrin, Elijah. Note that all these high achievers suffered from depression.

2. Request participants review Elijah's mountaintop experience from 1 Kings 18. Discuss the first activity of Day 2. Lead the class to assess why we may be prone to depression after a great success. Consider why Elijah was afraid of Jezebel after he'd just so powerfully defeated her favorite god. Ask: *Why did Elijah leave his servant behind? Why do we want to be alone when we're depressed? Why is that a mistake?* List and consider all the dark thoughts Elijah allowed to control him. Discuss the final activity of Day 2.

3. Invite participants to state the factors they think contributed to Elijah's state of depression. Note Dr. Pritchard's three diagnoses from Day 3. Ask how adults today get overstrained mentally. Help learners determine how we can know what our limits are. Ask: *What must we do when we realize we've reached our limit?* Discuss the first activity of Day 3. Invite participants to tell what they do to "come apart and rest awhile." Use the phrase "and when he saw" to explain how Elijah got out of touch spiritually. Ask: *How could Elijah have gone from such a spiritual high to being so completely out of touch? What must we do when we recognize our problems are looming so big they're blocking out God?*

4. Ask why many people, especially Christians, never acknowledge they are depressed. Ask: *Would depression be easier to handle if we recognized it's not a sin? Why?* Discuss question #1 of the final activity of Day 3. Ask: *How can depression and discouragement actually be God's merciful and gracious discipline?* Point out that Elijah had acknowledged he was no better than his ancestors. Perhaps after Mount Carmel he'd imagined himself the most powerful prophet of God who had ever lived.

Yet when a great national revival failed to materialize, he realized he was just human after all. Ask: *Why do we feel like we need to be better than others? Why might comparing ourselves to others, especially other family members, lead to depression?* Point out that our standards must be God's. Ask: *Do you think God is easier or harder on you than you are? Explain.* Discuss question #2 of the final activity of Day 3. Explain that Elijah and Moses were considered the greatest prophets of the Old Testament. To show Moses experienced a similar situation read aloud Numbers 11:10-15. Ask participants how they think God might respond to them if they spoke to Him that way. Read aloud God's response in Numbers 11:16-17. Emphasize to participants that God does not get mad at them when they are depressed! Invite someone to read aloud Psalm 34:18 from the margin of Day 4, page 64. Encourage learners who may be feeling depressed or discouraged to memorize that verse. ♥

5. Invite someone to read aloud 1 Kings 19:5-8. Lead the class to state ways God ministered to Elijah in his depression. Request participants silently complete the first activity of Day 4. Allow them to share ways they will give themselves a break. Ask a volunteer to read aloud 1 Kings 19:9-10. Consider reasons the Lord asked Elijah that question. Ask: *What usually makes it evident to you that you're throwing yourself a pity party? Why is self-pity the enemy of all spiritual growth?*

6. Ask participants how they usually respond to people who wallow in self-pity. Read aloud 1 Kings 19:11-13. Invite adults to state why they think it is significant God spoke to Elijah in a gentle whisper. Discuss the second activity of Day 5. Consider how we can hear God's gentle whisper. Ask someone to read aloud 1 Kings 19:14-18. Ask why a new commission might be the last thing we want but the greatest thing we need when we are depressed. Consider why it would be so encouraging for Elijah to hear of 7,000 faithful people. Note that this statement affirmed to Elijah that his service on Mount Carmel had not been worthless after all. Read aloud the final paragraph of Day 5. Allow time for learners to respond.

7. Close in prayer, asking God that learners will not give up but will realize that He loves them and is for them. ☯

Elisha Receives a Call

God's Call Forces Us to Make Difficult Choices

God was about to give Elijah a protégé, an apprentice, a young man whom he could mentor. God knew that Elijah needed a friend who could walk with him and share his burdens. He needed someone who could continue the work after he was gone.

Enter Elisha. When first we meet Elisha, he is plowing a field. But soon he will burn his plow, say farewell to his family, and give up his security to follow this wild mountain man wherever God leads him.

First there was Elijah.

Now there is Elisha.

Behind them both stands God.

Let us see what lessons we can glean from the calling of Elisha.

"So Elijah went from there and found Elisha son of Shaphat. He was plowing with twelve yoke of oxen, and he himself was driving the twelfth pair. Elijah went up to him and threw his cloak around him" (1 Kings 19:19, NIV).

It is not without significance that Elisha was plowing in the fields when Elijah threw his cloak around him. To us that simple act would have passed without meaning, but Elisha knew exactly what Elijah meant. A prophet's cloak was a distinctive garment, such as John the Baptist's cloak of camel's hair (Matt. 3:4). Placing a prophetic cloak on Elisha was like a king giving his scepter to his son. It was a sign of divine calling.

And where does Elijah find his man? In the field with 12 yoke of oxen (the sign of a wealthy family), with Elisha himself driving the twelfth pair. It wasn't as if Elisha were looking for a new job. Elisha had his hands full running the family farm. Ask those who grew up on a farm, and they will tell you the work never ends. Tending the animals, keeping the fields in shape, preparing to plant and harvest, dealing with the changing weather and the problems of your workers, juggling a thousand details every day—to keep on top of everything and do it all the time, you have to get up early and stay up late. Lazy men need not apply for the job. If you are a farmer, you live your work all day every day. I doubt that Elisha had any thought that before sundown he would slaughter his oxen and burn his plow. I'm sure that was nowhere on his radar screen when the day began.

But this is how God often works. He calls us when we are in the midst of our daily routine.

Read the following passages in your Bible. When did God call each person named:
Exodus 3:1-10, Moses: _____
1 Samuel 16:11-13, David: _____
Nehemiah 1:11-2:5, Nehemiah: _____
Matthew 4:18-20, Peter: _____
Matthew 9:9, Matthew: _____

God called Elisha when he was plowing the field. We are far more likely to encounter God by getting out of bed and getting busy doing our job than if we stay in bed waiting for a dream or a vision.

That leads to a profound insight: *99 percent of life is ordinary.* It's just the same old stuff day after day. You get up in the morning, take a shower, put on your clothes, eat breakfast, get the kids ready for school, go to work, hope the kids are OK, come back from work dead tired, read the paper, watch TV, try to be nice, eat supper, play with the kids, flop into bed dead tired, get up the next morning, and then do it all over again. That's the way life is. It's the same old thing day after day.

Where do you begin in discovering the will of God? *You begin by doing what you already know to be the will of God in your present situation.* So many of us live for those high mountain-peak experiences, for those times when the clouds part and God seems so close to us. Many people wish those spectacular moments would happen every day. Often when we say, "God, show me Your will," what we really mean is, "Lord, give me some feeling, some insight, some spiritual revelation." And God says, "I have already shown you My will. Now just get up and do it!"

- What is God's will for a student? God's will for a student is to do his or her homework.
- What is God's will for a doctor? Get up and do your rounds early in the morning.
- What is God's will for a pharmacist? Take extra care as you fill those prescriptions.
- What is God's will for a banker? Take care of the money entrusted to you.
- What is God's will for an accountant? Take care of those books, and do it right.
- What is God's will for a teacher? Do your lesson plans and come to class ready to teach.
- What is God's will for a salesman? Know your product, make your contacts, and move the merchandise.
- What is God's will for a football coach? Get your team ready to play the game on Friday night.
- What is God's will for an assembly-line worker? Show up on time, with a good attitude, ready to work.
- What is God's will for a flight attendant? Be on time and be in uniform with a smile on your face.

What is God's will for you? _____

(You may want to consult Col. 3:17,23, printed in the margin for your response.)

"And whatever you do, whether in word or deed, do it all in the name of the Lord Jesus, giving thanks to God the Father through him. . . . Whatever you do, work at it with all your heart, as working for the Lord, not for men" (Col. 3:17, 23, NIV).

So many of us want to live only on the mountaintop. That's not where you discover God's will. You discover God's will in the nitty-gritty of the valley every single day. The Bible says, "Whatever your hand finds to do, do it with all your might" (Eccles. 9:10). Why should God show you His will for the future if you aren't doing the will of God in the present?

Everything changed when Elijah showed up. No one had to tell Elisha who Elijah was. Everyone knew his name. People couldn't stop talking about how he called down fire from heaven and defeated the prophets of Baal. The whole nation knew about this strange, enigmatic, rough-hewn mountain man from Gilead who seemed to fear no one. He also seemed to appear and disappear without warning. No one knew where he was or what he was doing, and then bam! There he was again. Suddenly he showed up at Elisha's family farm, 300 miles from the cave on Mount Horeb.

It seems to have happened this way. Without a word Elijah strides up to Elisha, takes off his cloak, and puts it on Elisha. And then he begins to walk away. Elisha knew what it meant. Elijah was offering him a job. Now the young man had a choice to make. He could stay with the oxen, or he could follow the prophet's call. The life of a farmer was hard, but for Elisha it was also safe. He could stay with the oxen and keep plowing furrows, one after another, or he could walk away from all of it, into an unknown future which, if you consider the recent events on Mount Carmel, might get him into some hot water.

God has placed inside every man a desire to find an adventure to live. That's why men love fast cars, football, and movies like *Braveheart* and *The Dirty Dozen.* Men were born for adventure. We were hardwired by God to take risks; we were made to glance at our cards, look around the table, take a deep breath, and say, "All in." I'm not saying women don't do that because they do, but it's different because men and women are different. Elisha chose the hard path of risk instead of playing it safe. It's not like Elijah gave him a job description with fancy perks. Years ago I remember seeing a sign advertising for young people to join the California Conservation Corps. The sign read "Long Hours, Hard Work, Low Pay." That's pretty much the job description for a prophet. Elisha knew that going in, and he didn't hesitate.

day *Two*

God's Call Leads to Painful Separation

Read 1 Kings 19:20, printed in the margin. What did Elisha ask to do?

_____

"Elisha then left his oxen and ran after Elijah. 'Let me kiss my father and mother good-by,' he said, 'and then I will come with you.' 'Go back,' Elijah replied. 'What have I done to you?'" (1 Kings 19:20, NIV).

How does that indicate a painful choice to you?

_____

Here we come face-to-face with the high cost of following Jesus. I met a father and mother whose son serves Christ in a distant land. He is so far away from America that it took nine separate plane flights to reach a certain remote town in the jungle on the other side of the world. Once the parents got to that remote town, they had to take overland transportation to reach their son and his wife. The young couple literally have gone "to the ends of the earth" to bring the gospel to a tribe that knows nothing about Jesus. They have devoted themselves to learning the language, reducing it to writing, translating the New Testament, and someday learning to preach the good news in that language. They are doing this for the sake of 500 tribal people somewhere in the jungle on the far side of the earth. As I talked with the parents, I could sense the solemn joy mixed with sorrow at having their son and his wife so far away, living in the most primitive conditions. The parents miss their son and daughter-in-law terribly and rarely get to see them. But they offered their son to the Lord when he was born, and they have never gone back on that commitment. So there is sorrow and joy and solemn pride in their voices when they speak of him.

Read the various translations of Luke 14:26 printed in the margin. What must happen in your life if you are to answer God's call to go across town or across the world?

_____

This has always been part of the high cost of the Great Commission. If you follow Christ, you may end up in Tampa or Sacramento or Boston or Singapore. Who knows? You might end up in a ranch house in suburbia or a crowded apartment in Beijing. You might even get married and head for the jungle. Following Jesus has a price tag attached to it that we dare not disregard. And faithfulness to Christ may even lead us to do things that those closest to us will not understand or support.

"If you want to be my disciple, you must hate everyone else by comparison—your father and mother, wife and children, brothers and sisters—yes, even your own life. Otherwise, you cannot be my disciple" (Luke 14:26, NLT)

"If anyone comes to me but loves his father, mother, wife, children, brothers, or sisters—or even life—more than me, he cannot be my follower" (Luke 14:26, NCV).

"You cannot be my disciple, unless you love me more than you love your father and mother, your wife and children, and your brothers and sisters. You cannot come with me unless you love me more than you love your own life" (Luke 14:26, CEV).

Read Luke 18:29-30 in your Bible. What promise accompanies God's call to painful separation?

_____

Elisha would miss his family, and they would miss him. Nothing would ever be the same again. Never again would Elisha stand behind oxen while they plowed the field.

day Three

Elisha's Response

We learn several useful things from Elisha's response.

First, it was an immediate response. He left his oxen and ran after Elijah. Why did he run? Because Elijah wasn't staying around to discuss the matter. He placed his cloak on Elisha and then started walking away. Elisha ran because if he didn't, Elijah would soon have disappeared.

Second, it was a humble response. While Elisha accepts the call, he asks Elijah for permission to say farewell to his parents.

Third, it was a human response. He does not wish to disappear suddenly and leave his parents to wonder where he went and why. Elisha appears to have been a family man in the best sense of that word. Though God's call will now lead him into a new arena of activity, that departure is not to be accomplished without taking time to say farewell.

The purpose here is clear. Elisha is not going back to ask his parents for permission. He is old enough to respond on his own. But because he is a faithful son, he will not leave them in the lurch.

Read Luke 9:59-62, printed in the margin. What do you think these would-be disciples were trying to accomplish with their request?

_____

"[Jesus] said to another man, 'Follow me.' But the man replied, 'Lord, first let me go and bury my father.' Jesus said to him, 'Let the dead bury their own dead, but you go and proclaim the kingdom of God.' Still another said, 'I will follow you, Lord; but first let me go back and say good-by to my family.' Jesus replied, 'No one who puts his hand to the plow and looks back is fit for service in the kingdom of God'" (Luke 9:59-62, NIV).

What did Jesus assert with His answer?

_____

In that case the man meant, "Let me go home and stay with my father until he dies. When he is gone, then I will follow You." But such a reason is little more than an excuse cloaked in filial piety. The man never wanted to follow Jesus. Taking care of his father was just a pious excuse. Elisha is not like that at all. He wishes to say farewell to his family (as he should), and then he will gladly follow Elijah.

Read Mark 7:10-13 and John 19:25-27 in your Bible. What did Jesus obviously feel was the appropriate attitude and action toward one's family?

_____

God's call requires decisive action. "So Elisha left him and went back. He took his yoke of oxen and slaughtered them. He burned the plowing equipment to cook the meat and gave it to the people, and they ate. Then he set out to follow Elijah and became his attendant" (v. 21, NIV). You can't sit on the fence forever. Elisha had a few seconds to make a life-changing decision. Once he signed on to be Elijah's apprentice, he had to burn his bridges so that when things got tough, he wouldn't be tempted to go back to his old life.

That's why he slaughtered his oxen.

That's why he burned his plow.

day *Four*

Burn the Plow

Elisha slaughtered his oxen. He burned his plow. And he didn't do it in secret either. He threw himself a going-away party and invited everyone he knew. He cooked the meat from the oxen and then gave it to the people.

It was his way of saying, "The old life is gone forever. A new day has come for me."

Read 2 Corinthians 5:17, printed in the margin. What was the old that had gone and the new that had come for Elisha?

_____

> "Therefore, if anyone is in Christ, he is a new creation; the old has gone, the new has come!" (2 Cor. 5:17, NIV).

What is the old that has gone and the new that has come for you?

_____

Just as I typed those words, I thought of Billy Sunday, the famous baseball player turned evangelist. Billy Sunday lived a colorful life and experienced a dramatic conversion in 1886 at the Pacific Garden Mission in Chicago. As Billy himself told the story, he was standing outside a saloon with some of his teammates from the Chicago White Stockings (today called the Chicago Cubs) when a "gospel wagon" from the mission came down the street. Gripped with conviction of sin, he turned to his friends and said, "Boys, I've come to the end of the line. I'm through with the old life, and I'm heading in a new direction." That marked the turning point of his life. A few nights later after hearing Harry Monroe preach at the mission, Billy gave his heart to Christ. For the rest of his life, including his amazing evangelistic career in which he preached in person to 100 million people, he never tired of referring to the day he made a decision to follow Jesus.

When God calls, you have to make a decision. Elisha's burning of the plow takes on deep significance in light of Jesus' words in Luke 9:62, "No one who puts his hand to the plow and looks back is fit for service in the kingdom of God" (NIV).

It's not wrong to plow a field, but if your plowing keeps you from Jesus, you'd better burn the plow.

If you desire to dig deeper...

Examine negative examples of looking back in Genesis 19:15-26 and Numbers 14:1-4,26-35.

Why did the people in each instance look back?

What happened as a result?

What "plow" do you need to burn to follow Jesus?

_____

Anything good can become a hindrance if it keeps you from following the Lord. Elisha was saying, "I'm following God's call, and no matter what happens, I'm not going back. The old life is over forever. A new day has come for me."

day *Five*

The Hard Is What Makes It Good

Not long ago I watched (for the fifth or sixth time) *A League of Their Own,* starring Tom Hanks and Geena Davis. Near the end of the film, the team coached by Tom Hanks is about to play in the All-American Girls' Baseball World Series during World War II. Geena Davis, the star catcher, has decided to go home because her husband has returned from the war. Hanks confronts her by reminding her of how much she loves the game.

"I don't love it," she says, "not like you."

"Oh yes you do," Hanks replies. "It's in your blood."

"I can't do it," she says. "It's too hard."

At that moment Tom Hanks turns slightly, grabs his face, grimaces, and then says, "You're right. It is hard. It's supposed to be hard. The hard is what makes it good." With that he joins the rest of the team on the bus while Geena Davis leaves with her husband. Later she returns in time for the seventh and deciding game of the series.

"It's supposed to be hard. The hard is what makes it good."

That's not just true about baseball. That's the truth about the Christian life.

It is hard.

It's supposed to be hard.

The hard is what makes it good.

If it were easy, anyone could do it. But not everyone can. Not everyone can walk the Christ road.

The hard is what makes it good.

Read Matthew 7:13-14, printed in the margin.
Underline the destiny of all those on the easy road.
Circle the destination of those on the hard road.

"Enter through the narrow gate. For wide is the gate and broad is the road that leads to destruction, and many enter through it. But small is the gate and narrow the road that leads to life, and only a few find it" (Matt. 7:13-14, NIV).

If your name is Elisha and a mountain man throws his cloak on your back, you'd better follow him. But before you go, make sure you burn the plow so you can't go back when the going gets rough.

And it will get rough. It always does.

There will be hard days, bad days, sad days, discouraging days, confusing days, angry days, frustrating days, boring days, upsetting days, discombobulating days—and then there will be some really bad days.

The hard is what makes it good.

Stop your complaining. Stop your bellyaching. Stop your moaning. Stop dreaming of happier times and an easier road.

The hard is what makes it good.

Read Hebrews 10:38-39, printed in the margin.

What does it take to keep from shrinking back from that hard road?

_____

"But my righteous one will live by faith. And if he shrinks back, I will not be pleased with him. But we are not of those who shrink back and are destroyed, but of those who believe and are saved" (Heb. 10:38-39, NIV).

The good is better than you've ever dreamed. It's out of this world.

Pick up your cross and follow Christ. It's not easy, but it's not supposed to be easy.

Pick it up anyway. Follow Jesus. Go where He leads. It's the one decision you'll never regret.

Read Luke 9:23-24 in your Bible.

Why is it hard to follow Jesus? _____

Why is it good anyway? _____

Pray that God will strengthen you to be one who doesn't shrink back but presses forward in faith on the hard, but good, road.

To the Leader:

Has the Lord been impressing on you the need to "pass the mantle" on to someone else or at least to be training others to teach adults the Word of God?

Consider ways you can, like Elijah, throw your cloak over another person. Perhaps start small by asking such a person to lead a small group discussion within the class. You may ask him or her to research a particular topic and present it during the class session. Ask the person to teach in your absence. Invite him or her to attend a teacher training session with you.

Before the Session

1. Make six placards: 1. Do the Ordinary Well. 2. Accept the Cloak. 3. Be Humble. 4. Say Good-bye and Separate. 5. Burn the Plow. 6. Take the Hard Road.
2. If possible, obtain the movie clip referred to in Day 5. It can be found on YouTube "A League of Their Own, Part 10" Begin at 8:17 and end at 8:40 (that is, play 23 seconds).

During the Session

1. Ask: *What does it take to follow someone?* OR Ask two volunteers to follow you. Direct one volunteer to keep his or her eyes on you and the other volunteer to look backward while following you. After the demonstration, ask which volunteer was a better follower and why. FOR EITHER OPTION State that this week's lesson focuses on the man Elijah (and God) chose to follow him and eventually to succeed him as prophet. Adults can learn many lessons about how to be a good follower from Elisha.
2. Read aloud the first sentence of 1 Kings 19:19. Remind participants that last week they examined how God ministered to Elijah in his depression. As another act of mercy, God raised up someone to share the burden with Elijah and carry on his ministry when he was gone. Ask participants where they would look for someone to carry on such a brave, prophetic ministry. Read aloud all of 1 Kings 19:19. Consider why it's ironic yet significant that Elijah found his successor plowing a field. Ask participants if, in their experience, God has called them in a dramatic way or in the midst of their daily routine. Discuss the first activity of Day 1. Inquire: *What is the implication of the truth that 99 percent of life is ordinary?* State that the first lesson we can learn from Elisha about being a good follower is to do our ordinary jobs well. Display the first placard. Request someone to read aloud the verses from Colossians 3 in the margin of Day 1. Discuss how these verses can help us know the will of God for our lives. Invite volunteers to share their responses to the second activity of Day 1.

3. Explain the significance of Elijah's throwing his cloak around Elisha. Lead the class to consider why Elisha might have been tempted to throw off the cloak. Ask: *What "cloaks" of ministry might be thrown around us today? Why might we be tempted to throw them off?* State that the second lesson we can learn from Elisha about being a good follower is to accept the cloak. Display the second placard. Invite someone to read aloud 1 Kings 19:20. Consider ways Elisha demonstrated humility. [You may want to point out Elisha was from a wealthy family while Elijah was a mountain man whose family origins are unknown.] Ask why humility is a necessary attribute for a good follower. Display the third placard. ✋

4. Draw attention to the first three placards and ask participants if following seems particularly difficult so far. State: *Now we come to the hard and painful part of following.* Display and read aloud the fourth placard. Discuss the three activities in Day 2.

5. Discuss the first activity of Day 3. Consider why those would-be followers' requests were different from Elisha's—even if their wording was the same. Discuss the second activity of Day 3. Ask a volunteer to read aloud 1 Timothy 5:4,8. Guide the class to evaluate how Christians can balance the biblical command to care for one's family with Jesus' call to "hate" and leave one's family. Point out that we're never to abandon our families, but we are to say good-bye to things that are dear to us. Consider what adults may need to say good-bye to in order to follow Jesus. 🦶

6. Invite a volunteer to read aloud 1 Kings 19:21. Ask learners to state what Elijah was declaring when he burned his plow. Display the fifth placard. Discuss the first activity of Day 4. Invite someone to read aloud Philippians 3:7-14. Determine what "plows" Paul burned. Request participants silently consider the final activity of Day 4.

7. Describe the scene or show the clip from *A League of Their Own.* Display the sixth placard. Allow volunteers to share how they have discovered that "The hard is what makes it good." Use the activities in Day 5 to explore that truth. Close in prayer, asking God that the members of your class will not shrink back but press forward as faithful followers of Jesus Christ.

Payday Someday

day One

Meet the Main Characters

Three years have passed since the showdown on Mount Carmel. During those three years the people of Israel defeated the vastly superior Syrian army, which resulted in a period of peace and prosperity. But despite the slaughter of the prophets of Baal on top of Mount Carmel, it was still true that Ahab was the king; it was still true that wicked Jezebel was his wife. And as long as Ahab was the king and Jezebel was his wife, Baal worship would still grip the nation. But we have moved now three years down the road.

Ahab has his summer palace in a place called Jezreel. He has come to that palace for a few days of rest. One day Ahab is out walking, looking, and thinking. There next to the summer palace of Jezreel, nestled right up against it, is the vineyard of a man by the name of Naboth.

This story has four main characters. Let's meet them.

First is Naboth, a good and godly man, a man who worshiped the Lord and followed the law of his God. He was one of the 7,000 who had not bowed the knee to Baal. It happened that he owned a vineyard next to the summer palace of wicked king Ahab. So far as we know, prior to this Ahab had paid no attention to Naboth. But one day Ahab saw Naboth's vineyard and decided he wanted it. That covetous lust would set in motion a disastrous chain of events.

The second key player is Ahab. About him we need only say what we already have said, that no more wicked king ever sat upon the throne of Israel. Holy Scripture declares that he more than any other man imported the worship of Baal into Israel.

Read in your Bible 1 Kings 20:43 and 21:4-7. How would you describe Ahab's character?

_____

Ahab was the king, though I think it would be fair to say his life and his mind were really controlled by the third character in this story.

Her name is Jezebel. If Ahab was a wicked toad squatting on the throne of Israel, then Jezebel was an evil snake coiled around the throne. She was not an Israelite. She was a pagan woman out and out. She came from a long line of Baal worshipers in the Sidonian region of south Lebanon. When she married Ahab, she brought her wicked religion into Israel with her. And I suppose we should say this. Between Ahab and Jezebel, if you had to say who was worse, you would say that he was weak and she was strong. Ahab was easily influenced, and she was always ready to push her husband in the wrong direction.

Read 2 Kings 9:22, printed in the margin. What did the entire nation obviously know about Jezebel's character?

_____

"'How can there be peace,' Jehu replied, 'as long as all the idolatry and witchcraft of your mother Jezebel abound?'" (2 Kings 9:22, NIV).

And fourth, we have God's mountain man, Elijah the Tishbite. Since his great victory on Mount Carmel and his humiliating running away and going down to the cave in Mount Horeb, Elijah has not been heard from for three years. As far as we can tell, the man of God had made his last public appearance on top of Mount Carmel. Soon he will return to the public stage.

Based on previous studies, briefly describe Elijah's character.

_____

_____

day Two

The Story Unfolds

The story begins on that day in Jezreel when Ahab looked at the vineyard of Naboth and said to himself, "I'm the king of Israel. I need this vineyard, and I want this vineyard for myself." So Ahab went to Naboth and said, "Would you please sell your vineyard to me? If you will not sell your vineyard to me, would you please trade it? I am the king. If you will give me your vineyard, I will give you another piece of land here in Israel that is worth much more." I pause here to say the king was within his rights to do this. He did not sin by making that sort of offer. However, Ahab didn't count on the fact that Naboth was a man of God who followed the law of God. Naboth's simple reply to the king was: "The LORD forbid that I should give you the inheritance of my fathers" (1 Kings 21:3). One simple sentence. Those are the only recorded words of Naboth, but they tell us all we need to know: He was a man who respected the Lord; he was a man who respected the Lord's word; and he was a man who respected his own spiritual heritage.

Read Leviticus 25:23 and Numbers 36:7, printed in the margin. Why did Naboth refuse to sell his vineyard to Ahab?

_____

Naboth refused to sell the vineyard because if a family had been given a plot of land, it was to be handed down from father to son from generation unto generation. It was not to be sold. It was to be in the hands of the family forever. That was God's command. So Naboth said to the king, "The LORD forbid that I should do anything that should sully my family's inheritance and break the law of my God."

The king was upset, humiliated, and angry. He went back to his palace in a big funk. "So Ahab went home, sullen and angry because Naboth the

"The land must not be sold permanently, because the land is mine and you are but aliens and my tenants" (Lev. 25:23, NIV).

"No inheritance in Israel is to pass from tribe to tribe, for every Israelite shall keep the tribal land inherited from his forefathers" (Num. 36:7, NIV).

Jezreelite had said, 'I will not give you the inheritance of my fathers.' He lay on his bed sulking and refused to eat" (v. 4, NIV). The king threw a fit.

Read Deuteronomy 17:18-20 in your Bible. How was Ahab disobeying God's law even while Naboth faithfully obeyed the law?

_____

When the queen asked why he was so grouchy, he replied, "Because I said to Naboth the Jezreelite, 'Sell me your vineyard; or if you prefer, I will give you another vineyard in its place.' But he said, 'I will not give you my vineyard'" (v. 6, NIV). Ahab neglected to tell his wife the real reason Naboth would not sell—because he would not violate the law of God.

Jezebel had a plan. "Is this how you act as king over Israel? Get up and eat! Cheer up. I'll get you the vineyard of Naboth the Jezreelite" (v. 7, NIV). So wicked Jezebel hatched a diabolical plot. She decided to write a letter in the name of the king. She forged his name, although I suppose you can't really call it forgery because Ahab acquiesced in what she did. She composed the letter and had it sent to the elders of the town. The text of the letter she wrote is in the Bible. "Proclaim a day of fasting and seat Naboth in a prominent place among the people. But seat two scoundrels opposite him and have them testify that he has cursed both God and the king. Then take him out and stone him to death" (vv. 9–10, NIV). We call this a setup from the get-go. "So the elders and nobles who lived in Naboth's city did as Jezebel directed" (v. 11, NIV). The whole city had become so corrupt that the so-called spiritual leaders, instead of protesting this evil murderous plot, went along with Jezebel's plan.

We find out later in 2 Kings 9 that they also killed Naboth's two sons, thus leaving no living heirs, which meant the land now reverted to the crown. When Ahab learned that the land was his, he was pleased.

Who do you think was the most at fault for this travesty of justice—Ahab, Jezebel, or the elders of the town? Explain your response.

_____

"Yesterday I saw the blood of Naboth and the blood of his sons, declares the LORD, and I will surely make you pay for it on this plot of ground, declares the LORD" (2 Kings 9:26, NIV).

"Arise, Elijah"

It appears that the king and his wife had gotten away with murder. You say, "Where is God? Does He not know? Does He not care? Where is God when a man of God is killed for doing right? Where is God when the wicked rise to power? Where is God when a man like Ahab and a woman like Jezebel can get away with murder?"

Read Psalm 11 in your Bible. Where is God?

_____

What is He doing? _____

God came to His prophet, patted him on the shoulder, and told him to head for Jezreel. God said to Elijah: "Arise, prophet of God, I have a job for you to do." Three long years had passed since the last time the prophet had spoken publicly. I don't know if Elijah had wondered if God had put him on the shelf. Perhaps Elijah feared that his running away had caused God to give up on him. But God knew all along he had another job for His man. God was just waiting for the right time.

God told Elijah, "Go down to meet Ahab king of Israel, who rules in Samaria. He is now in Naboth's vineyard, where he has gone to take possession of it. Say to him, 'This is what the LORD says: Have you not murdered a man and seized his property?' Then say to him, 'This is what the LORD says: In the place where dogs licked up Naboth's blood, dogs will lick up your blood—yes, yours!'" (1 Kings 21:18–19, NIV).

When Elijah delivers his message, he adds an interesting phrase in verse 20: "I have found you . . . because you have sold yourself to do evil in the eyes of the LORD" (NIV). The Hebrew word translated "sold yourself" has a secondary meaning, "to marry." Elijah says to Ahab, "You have married evil, and in marrying evil you have given yourself completely to it."

Read 1 Kings 21:25-26, printed in the margin. How did Ahab marry evil literally and figuratively?

_____

"There was never a man like Ahab, who sold himself to do evil in the eyes of the Lord, urged on by Jezebel his wife. He behaved in the vilest manner by going after idols" (1 Kings 21:25-26, NIV).

There will be disaster in Ahab's family, his dynasty will come to an end, and dogs will consume Jezebel. The dogs will feed on those who die in the city, and the birds will eat the flesh of those who die in the country (vv. 20–24).

Elijah delivered the message, and then he disappeared. This seems to be a pattern with him. He just shows up, delivers his message, and then bam! He's gone.

Read in your Bible 1 Kings 21:27-29.
How did Ahab respond to Elijah's prophecy?

_____

Based on what you know about Ahab, do you think that lasted very long? Explain.

_____

day Four

Ahab Gets the Point and It All Goes to the Dogs

Days turned into weeks. Weeks turned into months. Ahab didn't hear from Elijah again. One day Ahab decided he wanted to go to war against Ben-Hadad, the king of Syria, the man he had defeated earlier. Only this time it was not going to work out so well. Ahab asked Jehoshaphat, the king of Judah, to join him in this war. Jehoshaphat agreed, and the day came when they were ready to go to battle. Knowing that he was a marked man, Ahab told Jehoshaphat to go to battle dressed as a king and he (Ahab) would go out dressed as a common soldier. What Ahab didn't know was that the king of Syria had told his army to concentrate only on killing Ahab. When the battle started, the Syrians spotted Jehoshaphat and were about to kill him, thinking he was Ahab. Suddenly someone shouted, "We've got the wrong king." In the confusion of battle, one of the Syrian archers saw the army of Israel and shot an arrow toward them at random. He wasn't aiming at anything. Ahab was dressed in armor like a regular soldier. The arrow just "happened" to come down and hit Ahab. The Bible says it hit between the sections of his armor. You could never do that on purpose. It's not even a million-to-one shot. That would be way too low. The soldier shot the arrow, and in the sovereign hand of God it went up, came down, and hit Ahab in the chink of his armor. He began to bleed profusely until the blood covered the floor of his chariot. But he would not leave the battlefield. When Ahab died that evening, the army began to scatter. They buried Ahab in Samaria and they took and washed out the chariot that was covered with his blood. When they washed out the blood, there was so much of it that the dogs came and licked it up, just as Elijah had predicted.

Jezebel Goes to the Dogs

Shortly after this Elijah was taken to heaven in a fiery chariot—as we will learn in next week's lesson. Five years pass. Ten years pass. Elijah's long gone. He's been replaced by Elisha. Jezebel is an older woman now. It seems as if Elijah was right about Ahab and wrong about Jezebel. You know where you have to find the rest of the story? You've got to turn all the way over to 2 Kings 9.

A military leader named Jehu became king of Israel. Like many others before him had done, he came to power by killing the reigning king, Joram, the second son of Ahab and Jezebel to rule Israel. When one of Elisha's prophets anointed Jehu as king, he gave Jehu a message from God to wipe out the house of Ahab (2 Kings 9:4–10). Jezebel still lived in the palace at Jezreel. So the Bible says Jehu got in his chariot and he made a little trip.

"Then Jehu went to Jezreel" (2 King 9:30, NIV). That's the summer palace. "When Jezebel heard about it, she painted her eyes, arranged her hair and looked out of a window" (v. 30, NIV). She may have thought she was going to seduce Jehu. Wrong. As Jehu entered the gate, she called out, "Have you come in peace?" (v. 31, NIV). It's the last thing she ever said.

Jehu looked up and called out, "Who is on my side?" (v. 32, NIV). Two or three eunuchs were standing near Jezebel. They served her; they knew her for what she was. So Jehu said, "Boys, I got a job for you. Grab that woman and throw her out." With pleasure, one imagines, they grabbed Jezebel; gave her the old one, two, three; and out the window she went, bouncing all the way down. Bam! She hit the ground hard. "They threw her down, and some of her blood spattered the wall and the horses as they trampled her underfoot" (v. 33, NIV). You know what this means? It means when they threw her body down, Jehu took his chariot and horses and ran over her again and again until she was absolutely, completely, totally dead.

A little while later Jehu said, "We can't leave that mess out there. Somebody go get her and bury her." So he sent his servants out, and they came back and said, "Well, we've got good news and bad news. The good news is she is still dead. The bad news is there's not much left. The dogs have come and licked up the blood. They have destroyed her body. Nothing is left except her skull, her feet and her hands."

Read 2 Kings 9:36 and 10:9-10, printed in the margin. What did Jehu recognize was the reason for such a gruesome occurrence?

"Jehu . . . said, 'This is the word of the LORD that he spoke through his servant Elijah the Tishbite: On the plot of ground at Jezreel dogs will devour Jezebel's flesh'" (2 Kings 9:36, NIV). "The next morning Jehu went out. He stood before all the people and said . . . 'Know then that not a word the Lord has spoken against the house of Ahab will fail. The Lord has done what he promised through his servant Elijah'" (2 Kings 10:9,10).

The Moral of the Story

What a story! Elijah had been in heaven for 10 years, but the word of the Lord came true. Let's focus on two important truths from this story.

First, God's patience will not last forever. Part of the gospel message is a message of judgment. The Lord is long-suffering and patient, not willing that any should perish but that all should come to repentance (see 2 Pet. 3:9). But there is a day of judgment coming for all of us. No one knows when that day will be, but there is a day for every man and woman and boy and girl. There's a day for every family, and there's a day for every nation. There is a day when God will finally say, "This far and no farther." God's patience will not last forever.

Second, God still looks for Elijahs who will stand up for him. We live in strange times. Morally confused times, days of religious and spiritual compromise. We need a generation of men and women who will have the

If you desire to dig deeper...

Read Revelation 2:20-25. What similarities do you see with Jezebel's life?

courage of their convictions and won't just deliver the good news but will have the courage to deliver the bad news too. We need someone to say to this dying generation, "Except you repent, you too will perish."

day *Five*

Elijah's Final Message

Now we must go back. This is the story of Elijah's last assignment.

God had one final job for his mountain man, and then he would take him home to heaven. The story begins this way: "After Ahab's death, Moab rebelled against Israel. Now Ahaziah . . ." (2 Kings 1:1–2, NIV). When Ahab died, his older son Ahaziah ascended to the throne of Israel. Remember that Jezebel was still alive. She lived for many more years. She was really the ruler of Israel. But one of Ahab's sons was sitting on the throne. He would only be on the throne for two short years, and then he would be gone. And it's the story of how he died that occupies our attention.

Ahaziah had fallen through the lattice of his upper room in Samaria and injured himself. We don't know how it happened. But when he hit the ground, he was evidently severely injured. And no one in all Israel could heal his injuries. So he thought to himself, *I need some help from above.* Only by *above* he wasn't thinking of the Lord God of Israel; he was thinking of someone else. "So he sent messengers, saying to them, 'Go and consult Baal-zebub, the god of Ekron, to see if I will recover from this injury'" (v. 2, NIV).

The name Baal-zebub appears only here in the Old Testament. Baal, of course, was the name of the false god that Jezebel had brought in. He was the god of the sun, the god of the storms, the god of fertility. The rest of the name means what it sounds like. Zebub actually gives you the sound zzzzzebub, it means the buzzing of flies. Baal-zebub literally means "lord of the flies." Baal-zebub was the particular name for the god of the people of the region of Ekron, a city located on the Mediterranean Sea. It was one of the five major cities of the Philistines. When they offered sacrifices to Baal-zebub, the Philistines believed he could predict the future. That's why Ahaziah wanted to consult Baal-zebub. He wanted to know if he would get better or if he was going to die from his injuries.

There is only one catch to this story. Israel already had a God, the Lord God of Israel. Instead of turning to the true God, Ahaziah put his future in the hands of Baal-zebub.

I don't criticize Ahaziah for wanting to know if he would recover. That's natural. *But he went to the wrong place.* That would prove to be a fatal mistake. We should not be surprised, because when people get desperate, they will turn to any source that promises them help—a friend on the phone, the psychic hotline, a horoscope, a medium, or a spiritualist.

Read the passages printed in the margin. What does God specifically tell His people not to do?

_____

What will God do if His people rebelliously disobey His command?

_____

We pick up the story again in verse 3: "But the angel of the LORD said to Elijah the Tishbite, 'Go up and meet the messengers of the king of Samaria and ask them, "Is it because there is no God in Israel that you are going off to consult Baal-zebub, the god of Ekron?"'" (NIV). Now comes the bad news for Ahaziah: "You will not leave the bed you are lying on. You will certainly die!" (v. 4, NIV).

Evidently the messengers were so disconcerted that they never made it to Ekron. They went back to the king with the report. The king wanted to know who dared give such a negative message. I love their answer because it's clear they had no idea who Elijah was. They described him this way: "He was a man with a garment of hair and with a leather belt around his waist" (v. 8, NIV). The king said, "I know that fellow. That was Elijah the Tishbite."

So the king sent out some men to capture Elijah. He sent out a captain with his company of 50 men. "The captain went up to Elijah, who was sitting on the top of a hill" (v. 9, NIV). Elijah is just sitting up there on the top of the hill, talking to the Lord. He's not hiding this time. He's out in the open where anybody can see him. And the captain of the 50 says, "Man of God, the king says, 'Come down.'" What do you think the king wants? The king wants to

"Do not turn to mediums or seek out spiritists, for you will be defiled by them. I am the LORD your God" (Lev. 19:31, NIV).

"I will set my face against the person who turns to mediums and spiritists to prostitute himself by following them, and I will cut him off from his people" (Lev. 20:6, NIV).

"Let no one be found among you who sacrifices his son or daughter in the fire, who practices divination or sorcery, interprets omens, engages in witchcraft, or casts spells, or who is a medium or spiritist or who consults the dead. Anyone who does these things is detestable to the LORD, and because of these detestable practices the LORD your God will drive out those nations before you" (Deut. 18:10-12, NIV).

"I will stretch out my hand against Judah and against all who live in Jerusalem. I will cut off from this place every remnant of Baal, the names of the pagan and the idolatrous priests … those who turn back from following the LORD and neither seek the LORD nor inquire of him" (Zeph. 1:4,6, NIV).

"Ignorant are those who carry about idols of wood, who pray to gods that cannot save … Who foretold this long ago, who declared it from the distant past? Was it not I, the LORD? And there is no God apart from me, a righteous God and a Savior; there is none but me. Turn to me and be saved, all you ends of the earth; for I am God, and there is no other. By myself I have sworn, my mouth has uttered in all integrity a word that will not be revoked: Before me every knee will bow; by me every tongue will swear. They will say of me, 'In the LORD alone are righteousness and strength.' All who have raged against him will come to him and be put to shame. But in the LORD all the descendants of Israel will be found righteous and will exult" (Isa. 45:20,21-25).

throw Elijah in jail. Elijah says, "If I am a man of God, may fire come down from heaven and consume you and your fifty men" (v. 10, NIV). That was the last thing the captain of the 50 heard because the next sentence says, "Then fire fell from heaven and consumed the captain and his men" (v. 10, NIV).

Evidently the king was a slow learner because he sent another captain with his 50 men to capture Elijah. Same story, second verse. Bam! Just like that, down came the fire consuming the second captain and the second 50 men (vv. 11–12).

So the king sent a third captain with his 50 men. I doubt they were volunteers. The third captain, who was smarter than the king, decided he didn't want to end up in flames. "This third captain went up and fell on his knees before Elijah. 'Man of God,' he begged, 'please have respect for my life and the lives of these fifty men, your servants! See, fire has fallen from heaven and consumed the first two captains and all their men. But now have respect for my life!'" (vv. 13–14, NIV).

The angel of the Lord told Elijah to go with him to see Ahaziah the king. It took a certain amount of courage to do that because Ahaziah's been told by the prophet he's going to die and 100 of his soldiers have died, consumed by fire. I'm sure Ahaziah was in a foul mood. I am sure Elijah knew that the king might try to put him to death at any moment. What do you think Elijah did? He didn't wait for Ahaziah to say a word. "This is what the LORD says: Is it because there is no God in Israel for you to consult that you have sent messengers to consult Baal-zebub, the god of Ekron? Because you have done this, you will never leave the bed you are lying on. You will certainly die!" (v. 16, NIV).

So the king died just as Elijah said he would. There are no details because it doesn't matter. He's gone. The only thing that really matters is the first part of verse 17: "So he died, according to the word of the LORD."

Yes, there is a God. He is the true and living God. You can turn to Him, you can trust Him, and you can count on His word.

As you read Isaiah 45:20-25, printed in the margin, underline truths that confronted and eventually destroyed Kings Ahab and Ahaziah. Bracket the lessons you have personally drawn from these episodes in Elijah's life.

During the Session

1. Ask: *Does patience indicate passiveness or power? Explain. When is it time for patience to give way to action?* OR Invite participants to state situations at home or work that push them to the limit so they finally say, "That's enough, I'm through putting up with this." Ask if they think God ever gets to that point and why.

2. Point out that God had patiently put up with Ahab and Jezebel's evil reign for a long time. But today participants will see Him say through Elijah, "That's enough. I'm through." The final straw occurred in a scenario that involved four characters. Use the remarks and the activities in Day 1 to identify and describe the four characters.

3. Invite someone to read aloud 1 Kings 21:1-3. Discuss the first activity of Day 2. Ask: *How did Naboth seal his fate with that simple sentence? What words would you use to describe Naboth—fool, faithful, naïve, brave? Explain.* Request a volunteer read aloud 1 Kings 21:4-16. Call for responses to the final activity of Day 2. Discuss why some people might say God was to blame for the terrible action taken against Naboth and his family.

4. Read aloud the first paragraph of Day 3. Invite participants to state other questions they have when it looks like evil is winning and God is not acting. Discuss the first activity of Day 3. Read aloud 1 Kings 21:17-24. Consider reasons this episode with Naboth was the final straw that led God to say, "I'm through with you, Ahab." Ask participants to turn in their Bibles to Proverbs 6:16-19. Read these verses. Evaluate how Ahab and Jezebel embodied all seven attitudes and actions that God hates. Complete the last activity of Day 3. Ask if learners were surprised at Ahab's response. Inquire: *Do you think it's fair that God softened Ahab's punishment? Why?* Explain that God always keeps His word. All that was spoken to Ahab would come true; however, Ahab would not see the complete disaster of his entire family being wiped out—that would occur over 10 years later (see 2 Kings 10). 🎧

5. Explain that 2 Kings 22:1-28 covers three years of Israel's history. Ask: *What do you think Ahab felt every time he heard a dog bark during*

To the Leader:

Today's lesson covers many passages of Scripture and many years of history. Take time this week to read in its entirety 1 Kings 20–22 and 2 Kings 1,9–10.

Be prepared to relate these events in an interesting manner so participants can see how God worked through real people in history. As you help learners grasp historical events, be certain to keep the main focus on encouraging them to apply the biblical truths in those stories to their own lives.

those three years? Elijah seems to have been quiet and absent during those three years while Ahab appears to have gone back to his arrogant, godless ways. Ahab wanted once again to go to war against the king of Syria whom he'd earlier defeated. When another godly prophet, Micaiah, foretold disaster if he went to war, Ahab had him thrown into prison. Invite someone to pick up with the rest of the story by reading aloud 1 Kings 22:29-38. Invite participants to state evidences from this passage that God obviously was in complete control.

6. State that 10 years pass, Elijah goes to heaven, Elisha takes over the ministry, and a son of Ahab named Joram becomes king. Summarize 2 Kings 9:1-10. Ask someone to read aloud 2 Kings 9:30-37. Discuss the activity of Day 4. Ask: *Do you think Jezebel got what she deserved? Do you wonder why she was allowed to live so much longer before she got her punishment? Why?* Ask someone to read aloud 2 Peter 3:8-9. Ask how these verses help participants understand how God is being just when it seems it's taking a long time for Him to execute judgment on wicked people. Inquire: *Why should we be thankful God is patient with evil people?* Request someone read aloud 2 Peter 3:10-14. Ask: *What can we be certain about even though God is so patient?* Discuss: *What implications does that have for us as God's people?*

7. Remind participants you skipped forward many years to see Elijah's prophecy against Jezebel fulfilled. Now you're backing up to examine Elijah's final assignment. Invite someone to read aloud 2 Kings 1:1-8. Consider reasons Ahaziah preferred to consult the god of Ekron than the God of Israel. Discuss: *What do people today, even Christians, turn to for answers instead of God? Why do they do that?* Discuss the first activity of Day 5. Explore why God is so opposed to us turning to anything other than Him for guidance and wisdom. Briefly summarize the rest of the story in 2 Kings 1:9-17. Discuss the final activity of Day 5. Ask: *What is the only logical response to God's long-suffering but limited patience?* Close in prayer. 🎧

Chariots of Fire

day One

Elijah's Last Day

What would you do if you knew that you were going to die today?

What if you knew with absolute certainty that today was going to be your last day on earth? Suppose you had less than 24 hours to live. What would you do? Where would you go? Would you stay where you are right now, or would you hop on a plane and go see someone you love? Would you pick up the phone and call a few people? If you did, whom would you call? What would you say?

That brings us to the last chapter in Elijah's story. From 2 Kings 2 we learn how a man of God leaves this earth well. Elijah doesn't die, but the way he spends his last day is a message to us all.

On the last day of Elijah's earthly life, he does a lot of walking. He starts in Samaria and goes to Gilgal. From Gilgal he goes to Bethel. From Bethel he goes down to Jericho. From Jericho he goes to the east side of the Jordan River. His final walk takes him back to the hills and ravines of his boyhood. God's mountain man returns to the mountains from whence he came. Amid those lonely rocky hills and deep gullies, the prophet prepares to meet the Lord. Depending on the roads you take, that's at least 40 to 55 miles. That's quite a bit of walking in one day. So whatever else you want to say, don't say Elijah was out of shape. He was obviously in excellent shape. Don't say he was taken to heaven because he was old and tired and worn out because Elijah still had plenty of vitality on his last day. He took this long walk because God had told him today was going to be the day.

Do you believe God sometimes gives His children a little advance notice that heaven is not far away? I do. But I imagine most of us could tell a story of a saint of God who had some premonition that heaven was not far away. We hear stories of angels singing, of bright lights, of the vision of the glory of Christ. While I don't think we should be gullible and believe everything people say, I don't think that we should discount all those stories.

Read Acts 7:55-60 in your Bible. What did Stephen see right before he died?

_____

I believe that sometimes God allows us to hear the sound of the chariot swinging low to carry us home. God in His grace sometimes allows His children to know that the day has arrived.

Read 2 Kings 2:1-6 in your Bible. List in the margin all who knew that day would be Elijah's last day on earth.

It's also clear that Elisha, his young protégé, also knew this was the final day. And it's clear that God had told the company of the prophets in these different towns. That explains why Elijah would do all that walking on his last day. It also answers a question that has been left hanging in the air. What was Elijah doing during those long stretches when he suddenly disappeared from view? Now we know the answer. Elijah obviously had spent a great deal of his time building into other people. In Gilgal and Bethel and Jericho (and probably other cities and towns as well), Elijah had set up little hometown seminaries where prophets could be trained for the ministry. He understood that his greatest gift to the nation would be to multiply himself by leaving behind a crop of young men who could carry on his work after he was gone. One man could only do so much, but one man who poured himself into dozens of younger men could start a movement that might one day ignite a revolution that could overthrow Baal worship once and for all. Here is the ultimate argument for Christian education. We pass along what we know to the up-and-coming generation precisely because we know we won't be here forever. We do it so that our work will not end when we do, but in the providence of God, while we sink into the dust of the earth, God's truth goes marching on.

Read the passages from 2 Timothy and Titus printed in the margin. What did Paul the apostle expect of these two young men whom he had mentored?

_____

"And the things you have heard me say in the presence of many witnesses entrust to reliable men who will also be qualified to teach others" (2 Tim. 2:2, NIV).

"The reason I left you in Crete was to … appoint elders in every town…. For an overseer, as God's manager, must be blameless, not arrogant, not quick tempered, not addicted to wine, not a bully, not greedy for money, but hospitable, loving what is good, sensible, righteous, holy, self-controlled, holding to the faithful message as taught, so that he will be able both to encourage with sound teaching and to refute those who contradict it" (Titus 1:5,7-9, HCSB).

These young prophets loved Elijah and looked to him as their guide, mentor, hero, and friend. In Gilgal and Bethel and Jericho, everywhere he went that last day, the school of the prophets was dismissed. The young prophets who were trained by the older prophets came out to see the man of God as he made his farewell tour. God had not only told Elijah and Elisha; he also told the other prophets in Israel, "The man of God is going home today."

Elijah knew today was the day. But I don't think he knew exactly when it was going to happen or where or how. I don't know that he had any inkling of being carried to heaven in a whirlwind. So Elijah now has Elisha with him. When he comes to Gilgal, he says, "Stay here." And Elisha says, "No, I'm going with you." When he comes to Bethel, he says, "Stay here." Elisha says, "No, I'm going with you." When he comes to Jericho, he says, "Stay here." "No, I'm going with you." When he comes to the Jordan, he says, "Stay here." "No, I'm going with you." It was a test of loyalty and a test of tenacity. It was Elijah's way of saying to Elisha, "I'm about to leave you. Can you handle it?" And Elisha is saying to his mentor, "Wherever you go I will go. I will be with you to the very end." It's a touching picture of the older man and the younger man and the final test of loyalty.

So Elijah spent his final day with Elisha, and he spent his time greeting and saying farewell to the young prophets who looked up to him as a hero and a mentor.

There is no sense of panic here. Elijah was not afraid; Elisha was not afraid. There's no sense of fear or dread, just a sense of being completely in God's hands.

day Two

Elijah's Last Words

When they came to the Jordan River, Elijah took his cloak, rolled it up, and struck the water. The water parted, showing yet one more time how Elijah and Moses were both filled with the Spirit of God. Just before Elijah left for heaven, he turned and said to his young friend, "What can I do for you? Before I go, do you have any last requests?" And Elisha said, "Let me inherit a double portion of your spirit" (2 Kings 2:9, NIV).

If you could inherit a double portion of someone's spirit, whose spirit would you choose? _____

How would having that person's spirit affect how you thought and behaved?

_____

When Elisha asked for a double portion of Elijah's spirit, he was revealing the priorities of his life. In the Old Testament the oldest son received a double portion of his father's estate. Elisha was not literally the physical son of Elijah, but he was his spiritual son. So as the oldest son spiritually he was asking, "Oh my father, give me what belongs to me spiritually. Grant me a double portion of your spirit." Why did he ask for that? Those were hard days in the nation of Israel, and soon matters would get worse. Instead of getting better in the days of Elisha, the people continued to turn away from God. Elisha knew that in order for him to serve the Lord in the hard, difficult days ahead, he needed the same courage and the same resolve and the same fortitude and the same boldness that his master had had. He wanted the same spirit that Elijah had on top of Mount Carmel. He wanted the same spirit that caused him to go before Ahab in the first place. He wanted the same spirit that Elijah had had when he faced down Ahaziah. He wanted that, and he knew he needed it. God bless Elisha for realizing the need in his own life.

Elijah said back to him, "You have asked a difficult thing" (v. 10, NIV). It was a gift only God could give. Then he added an important condition: "If you see me when I am taken from you, it will be yours—otherwise not" (v. 10, NIV).

Now we come to the end of Elijah's earthly life. "As they were walking along and talking together, suddenly a chariot of fire and horses of fire appeared" (v. 11, NIV). Those are military images. The horses and the chariot were symbols of battle. Elijah was a warrior for God. It was a sign and a symbol that there was a battle raging for the hearts of people of Israel. It meant that a warrior was about to come home to God. It's a symbol of the kind of life Elijah has led. "Elijah went up to heaven in a whirlwind" (v. 11, NIV). Elijah's life had been a whirlwind of activity. He had been so impetuous, so driven, so determined, thrusting himself into the palace of ungodly kings, blowing through Israel like a tornado from God. He left the earth as he lived on the earth—in a whirlwind.

We tend to focus on the spectacular departure, but verse 12 matters more: "Elisha saw this" (NIV). Fifty prophets followed at a distance. They saw Elijah and Elisha together, and suddenly Elijah disappeared. I think it means that all they saw was Elijah disappear. They had no idea what had happened. It was only Elisha whose eyes were opened to see the flaming horses and the flaming chariot. It was only Elisha who saw his master being taken away in the whirlwind. "If you see me," Elijah said. There is the kind of seeing with the eyes, and there is the seeing with the eyes of the heart. It is possible to have 20/20 vision on the outside and be totally blind on the inside. You can live 80 years with perfect vision and be totally blind to spiritual reality. That's why Paul prays in Ephesians 1:18 that the "eyes of your heart may be enlightened." You could go to Sunday School all your life, you could even attend a Christian college or go to seminary, and the eyes of your heart could be tightly shut. Just going through the motions doesn't guarantee the eyes of your heart will be open.

**Read Matthew 13:13-15, printed in the margin.
What's involved in truly seeing?** _____

What keeps people from truly seeing? _____

Elijah said, "You can have the power if you see me depart." He didn't just mean if you visually see me, but if God gives you spiritual sight to understand, if He opens the eyes of your heart.

How do I know God answered that prayer? Not because Elisha parted the Jordan with Elijah's cloak (2 Kings 2:13–14). I know it because of the wonderful story that takes place in 2 Kings 6:8–17 when Elisha and his servant are in Dothan and the armies of the king of Aram have completely surrounded them. It's a hopeless situation. Though the servant despairs, Elisha tells him not to worry because "those who are with us are more than those who are with them" (v. 16, NIV). Then Elisha prays, "O LORD, open his eyes so he may see" (v. 17, NIV). When his eyes were opened,

"This is why I speak to them in parables: 'Though seeing, they do not see; though hearing, they do not hear or understand.' In them is fulfilled the prophecy of Isaiah: 'You will be ever hearing but never understanding; you will be ever seeing but never perceiving. For this people's heart has become calloused; they hardly hear with their ears, and they have closed their eyes. Otherwise they might see with their eyes, hear with their ears, understand with their hearts and turn, and I would heal them'" (Matt. 13:13-15, NIV).

the servant saw the armies of God arrayed in the clouds above the Aramean army. It is a great advance spiritually to have your eyes opened to see spiritual reality, to understand that this world is not the only world. When the eyes of the heart are opened, you understand that the unseen world is the real world, the only one that matters.

Read Matthew 13:16-17, printed in the margin. Write in the margin a prayer, thanking God for the blessing of spiritual vision.

day *Three*

Elijah's Lasting Legacy

So now one prophet is taken and one prophet is left, showing us that the battle goes on. The church triumphant rejoices in heaven while the church militant on earth continues the battle.

Elisha saw spiritual reality. He saw behind the scenes. At the end of the story, three things happen in quick succession:

1. Elisha saw Elijah depart.
2. Elisha picked up Elijah's cloak.
3. Elisha took the cloak to the Jordan River, and he said, "Where is the Lord, the God of Elijah?"

Why did Elisha do that? Elisha was on the east bank of the Jordan.

Read 2 Kings 2:11-14 in your Bible. Record in the margin the question Elisha asked when he took the cloak to the river.

Elisha had to get across to enter into God's assignment for his life. There was no better time than the present to find out if God would be with him as he had been with Elijah. Don't you think it took courage to take that cloak and hit the Jordan River? Elisha had seen Elijah separate the waters, but would the same thing happen for him? Elijah is gone, but is Elijah's God gone also? That's always the great question.

Read Hebrews 13:5,8, printed in the margin. What is God's consistent answer to that great question?

_____

"God has said, 'Never will I leave you; never will I forsake you.' … Jesus Christ is the same yesterday and today and forever" (Heb. 13:5,8, NIV).

It took faith to take that same cloak and hit the water, not knowing what was about to happen. It took courage to do that. It was necessary. Elisha had to do it.

It is the same in every generation. Leaders rise, lead, fight the battle for God, and then at the appointed hour, they move off the scene to be replaced by others whom God has raised up.

Read Numbers 27:12-23 in your Bible. Which godly leader was moving off the scene? _____
Whom did God raise up to take his place? _____
What similarities do you see between this passage and the transfer of leadership from Elijah to Elisha?

_____

day *Four*

God Names His Own Successors

Now we come to the final turn in the road. *Elijah is in heaven, and he's alive and well today.* Hundreds of years later the Lord said through Malachi, "I will send you the prophet Elijah before that great and dreadful day of the LORD comes." (Mal. 4:5, NIV). Four hundred years later, Jesus said of John the Baptist, "He is the Elijah who was to come" (Matt. 11:14, NIV). He meant that John the Baptist had come in the spirit and power of Elijah (Luke 1:17). And later Elijah appeared on the Mount of Transfiguration with Jesus, Peter, and John (Mark 9:2–8). That means he is still alive today.

So if this were your last day, how would you spend it? What would you do? For those who know the Lord, death holds no fear. Our little time on planet Earth zips by, and then we fly away. We're here today and gone tomorrow. Here is the wonderful final word from Elijah's life.

Elijah went to heaven.

Elisha carried on his work.

God's work goes on.

God's work goes on because God goes on.

God was here before we arrived, and He will be here long after we are gone. Nothing of God dies when a man of God dies.

"Nothing of God dies when a man of God dies."—Ray Pritchard

"For the LORD is good and his love endures forever; his faithfulness continues through all generations" (Ps. 100:5, NIV).

Read Psalm 100:5, printed in the margin. Check those of your family God will care for long after you're gone.

❑ **Your children**
❑ **Your grandchildren**
❑ **Your great grandchildren**
❑ **Your great great grandchildren**

How can you know that? _____

When Elijah went to heaven, God was still the same. When Elisha died, God was still the same.

Elijah departs for heaven.

Elisha picks up Elijah's mantle and carries on his work.

God names His own successors.

The Lord God of Elijah is also the Lord God of Elisha.

We come and go, but our God spans the generations.

Where is the Lord God of Elijah? I've got good news for you. He's still here. The first words out of Elijah's mouth were "As the LORD, the God of Israel, lives" (1 Kings 17:1, NIV). The Lord God of Elijah is our God today.

So I leave you with the question that I started with. Where is the Lord God of Elijah? He's still here. But where are the Elijahs of the Lord God in our own generation?

Read 2 Timothy 4:1-7 in your Bible.
Why do we still need Elijahs in our world today?

_____

What does God require of this generation's Elijahs?

_____

day *Five*

Conclusion

As we wrap up our journey through the life of God's mountain man, let's pause to consider two facts about Elijah from the New Testament. *First, Elijah was a lot like us.* When James wanted to encourage his readers to pray fervently, he used this illustration: "Elijah was a man just like us. He prayed earnestly that it would not rain, and it did not rain on the land for three and a half years. Again he prayed, and the heavens gave rain, and the earth produced its crops" (Jas. 5:17–18, NIV).

In the margin state how you saw yourself in this eight-week study of Elijah.

The *King James Version* says that Elijah was a man of "like passions." It means that Elijah was not some superhuman man in a category far beyond the rest of us mere mortals. Elijah experienced all the emotions of life—joy, sorrow, victory, defeat, frustration, exultation, encouragement, discouragement, anger, forgiveness, despair, and relief. We face a twofold danger when we study a life of great accomplishment. On the one hand we tend to canonize a man, treating him as if he were exempt from the normal temptations of life. It is easy to chisel Elijah's head on some religious Mount Rushmore and say, "There never was such a man before or since." Or we may focus on a great man's weaknesses and infirmities, concentrating on his failures, faults, and foibles, exposing every sin and every foolish mistake so that in the end he seems not very great at all. We pull him down into the muck and mire of ordinary life until the luster of his greatness has disappeared underneath the veneer of his frailty. All the heroes of the Bible had their weaknesses, and Elijah was no exception. And that is one reason we are drawn to such a man. God used him in spite of his weaknesses.

There is one final thought we need to keep in mind. *Elijah was a lot like Jesus.* At first glance that may seem wrong because Elijah made mistakes and Jesus was sinless. But consider this. Elijah and Jesus were both sent by God. Both were misunderstood by their contemporaries. Both spent time alone in the wilderness. Both worked miracles. Both men spoke the truth. Both of them riled the religious and political establishment of their day. Both of them ascended into heaven—Elijah in a whirlwind and Jesus rising through the clouds. It should not surprise us that some of the common people thought Jesus was the second coming of Elijah (Matt. 16:13) or that when Jesus cried out on the cross, some thought He was calling for Elijah (Matt. 27:47). Nor should we be surprised that Elijah appeared along with Moses during the transfiguration (Matt. 17:3).

No wonder the Jews revere Elijah. There never was another man like him. He stands alone in biblical history. Though he lived hundreds of years before Christ, he lived and ministered in the power of the Lord. Study Elijah, learn to be like him, follow his steps, and he will lead you to Jesus.

Elijah was one man wholly dedicated to God in a generation when most people were dedicated to evil. Though far from perfect, he left a mark the world remembers almost 3,000 years later. He did what he could, while he could, and he did not shirk his duty. When he had a chance to make a difference, he did. And he didn't worry too much about who was with him and who was against him. He figured that one man plus God was enough—and he was right.

What a man!

What a God he served!

Elijah still speaks today because Elijah's God still lives today.

How has this study of Elijah spoken to you personally?

During the Session

1. Ask: *What would you do if you knew you were going to die today?* OR Write on the board "I would ..." and "I would not ..." Lead the class to make a list of 10 things they would and would not do if they knew they had a set amount of days left to live. FOR EITHER OPTION State that the class is going to examine Elijah's last day on earth. Point out that from his example participants can learn how to live well and leave well.

2. Invite someone to read aloud 2 Kings 2:1-6. If possible, point out the locations mentioned on a map. Ask why Elijah would do so much walking on his last day on earth. Indicate that he was visiting people who meant a great deal to him. Explain the purpose of the companies of prophets. State that the meaningful way Elijah spent his last day on earth revealed that he'd lived other days meaningfully as well. Discuss the third activity in Day 1. Brainstorm ways participants can build into the lives of others.

3. Point out that Elijah was also visiting significant places. Request a volunteer read aloud Joshua 4:19-24. Explain that Gilgal signified the beginning of the Hebrews' occupation of the promised land of Canaan. Ask: *Why is it valuable for us to occasionally go back to the beginning of our relationship with God?* Invite someone to read aloud Genesis 28:16-18. Lead learners to consider how revisiting our "Bethels"—places we encountered God—empowers us to live and die well. Invite participants to recall what significant event occurred at Jericho (Josh. 6). Ask and then discuss: *What were Elijah's Jerichos—that is, places of his great battles and victories? What are your Jerichos? How does recalling those victories won by God help you live well?* Request a volunteer read 2 Kings 2:7-8. Explore the significance of the Jordan River being Elijah's final location. State: *We all have to cross the river at some point. We can, like Elijah, cross with peace and power or we can cross with fear and fighting. What makes the difference?*

4. Invite someone to read aloud 2 Kings 2:9-10. Examine how Elijah's request revealed his priorities. Discuss the first activity of Day 2. Request someone read aloud 2 Kings 2:11-12. Allow participants to

To the Leader:

Pray Ephesians 1:18-19 for each learner by placing his or her name in the blanks:

"I pray that the eyes of _____'s heart may be enlightened in order that _____ may know the hope to which God has called _____, the riches of His glorious inheritance, and His incomparably great power for us who believe."

Make contact with learners, letting them know you prayed that prayer for them.

state what they think is the significance of Elijah being taken up in a whirlwind. Point out that Elijah's extraordinary departure marked him as an extraordinary prophet. Because he didn't actually die he became the symbol of future prophets. To demonstrate this, ask someone to read aloud the final two verses of the Old Testament in Malachi 4:5-6.

5. Remind participants that 50 men were watching from the other side of the Jordan when Elijah ascended. Have learners reflect on why Elisha was the only one who saw Elijah leave in the whirlwind. Discuss the second activity of Day 2. Ask what it takes to have 20/20 spiritual vision. Urge participants to pray for God to open the eyes of their hearts. Remind learners of songs that voice that prayer. These may include such hymns as "Open the Eyes of My Heart" (No. 66), "Open Our Eyes, Lord" (No. 426), and "Open My Eyes, That I May See" (No. 443). [All hymns suggestions and numbers are from LifeWay's new *Baptist Hymnal* (Nashville: LifeWay Worship, 2008).]

6. Invite someone to read aloud 2 Kings 2:13-14. Ask: *What question did Elisha ask? Do you think he asked it? with fear? with faith? with uncertainty? Explain. Why did Elisha need an answer to that question? What was God's answer?* Invite volunteers to share when they've basically asked the same question Elisha did. Complete the second activity of Day 3.

7. Request someone read aloud the quotation in the margin of Day 4. State that when one person's work is finished another person's work is just beginning. The reason for this is because God names His own successors. Use the Scriptures from the final activities of Days 3 and 4 to identify and discuss Moses' and Paul's successors. Explore: *Why does one leader have to go for another leader to rise? Do you think Joshua, Elisha, or Timothy would have fully developed their own faith or discovered their own God-given power if Moses, Elijah, and Paul had remained? Why or why not? What does this say to us as adult children of Christian parents? What does it say to us as parents?* Discuss the final activity of Day 4.

8. Use the activities in Day 5 to help adults review what they have gained from this study of Elijah.

9. Close in prayer, asking God that Elijah's life will continue to challenge participants to be risk-takers so they can become all God wants them to be.

10. Announce the new study "Landmines in the Path of the Believer" from Charles Stanley that begins next Sunday.

Dr. Charles Stanley

has been Senior Pastor of First Baptist Church in Atlanta, Georgia, since 1971. He is also the founder and president of *In Touch Ministries*, a radio and television program that can be heard around the world in more than 100 languages. He has written more than 50 books, including *Living the Extraordinary Life, When the Enemy Strikes, Finding Peace, God Is in Control, Pathways to His Presence, Success God's Way, Handbook for Christian Living, The Source of My Strength, How to Listen to God*, and *Life Principles Bible*.

MARGARET DEMPSEY-COLSON is a graduate of the University of Georgia and the New Orleans Baptist Theological Seminary. She and her husband have taught Sunday School at First Baptist Church, Marietta, Georgia, for several years. Margaret enjoys travel and long-distance running.

ABOUT THIS STUDY

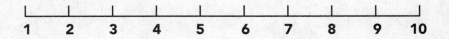

Read 1 Peter 5:8. How aware are you of the adversary in your life? _____

How do you think you could be more spiritually alert?

_____

On a scale of 1 to 10, rate yourself in walking wisely, understanding and following God's will?

1	2	3	4	5	6	7	8	9	10

Landmines in the Path of the Believer

If you have accepted Jesus Christ as your Savior, then you need to know that the enemy will stop at nothing to prevent you from knowing God and living for Jesus Christ. His most devastating weapons of warfare lay hidden below the surface of our spiritual landscape. When we step on one of the enemy's landmines, the explosion that follows usually has an adverse effect on our relationships with God and with others, as well as on our personal testimony. Sometimes the injury seems beyond repair, but it never is when God is involved.

You may feel as though you are standing in a minefield right now and you do not know which way to turn. I want to assure you that God knows. He has a plan for your rescue. No matter how great the temptation, you can take back any spiritual ground you have given to the enemy and reclaim your rightful position as a child of God.

The one thing that exposes, unearths, and disarms any landmine left in the path of a believer is truth—God's truth. Throughout this study you will be given key principles that can help you discover how to live a victorious Christian life without compromising what you know God has given you to do. When we can practice the principles written in His Word, we experience true freedom from sin, shame, and guilt.

This is my prayer for you—that God will show you how to uncover and protect yourself from the enemy's destructive weapons, such as disappointment, pride, jealousy, compromise, fear, and more, and that you will reach your full potential as a child of God.

Charles Stanley

Hidden Threats

day One

Face-to-Face with Our Enemy

Those who have fought the good fight of faith will tell you that when you are in the heat of a spiritual battle, it does not take long to realize Satan will do anything to prevent you from becoming the person God has planned for you to be. Although God never wants us to fear the enemy's threats, a key step to spiritual victory comes when we acknowledge we have an enemy who poses a real threat.

Satan's strategic plan is laid out to entice you to sin and to drift in your devotion to God. How does he do this? He uses many of the things we feel are harmless or unavoidable sins—gossip, feelings of unforgiveness, pride, and cynicism, to name a few. He also watches to see how we will react to a situation. If there is an opportunity for him to weave his evil mischief into our thoughts, he will take it.

The landmines in his arsenal include such sins as pride, jealousy and envy, disappointment, unforgiveness, compromise, sexual temptation, fear, and laziness—which God also calls slothfulness. When you and I step on a landmine, an explosion occurs. We may not immediately know the extent of the damage, but we can predict it will affect our lives in countless ways. This is the reason we need to know how to detect, identify, and protect ourselves from the destruction that comes as a result of the enemy's landmine tactics.

Wars are not won by rushing into battle without a plan or a map of the combat zone. Likewise, God does not intend for us to go through life blindly—failing to consider the consequences of our actions and the responsibility we have been given as believers. Paul cautioned us to "walk, not as unwise men but as wise, making the most of your time, because the days are evil. So then do not be foolish, but understand what the will of the Lord is" (Eph. 5:15-17).

You may be shaking your head and wondering how in the world you could ever hope to stay in tune with God's will, especially when temptation is ready to throw you off the path at every turn. The truth is, at some point, all of us have wondered how we can say no to something that appears so innocent yet contains deadly potential.

What are the temptations that personally challenge you to veer off the path of God's will?

_____

_____

If you desire to dig deeper:

Look up these passages and make note of the encouragement you find.
• **Lamentations 3:22-23**
• **Ephesians 6:10-13**
• **Philippians 4:13**

God has promised to be our strength in times of difficulty, heartache, and brokenness. However, you must settle two things. First, God is greater that any weapon Satan can bring against you. No matter how horrendous Satan's attack may seem, God is all-powerful. Second, to conquer these sins, you must acknowledge that God has forbidden each one.

Oswald Chambers writes, "When once the light breaks and the conviction of wrong comes, be a child of the light, and confess, and God will deal with what is wrong; if you vindicate yourself, you prove yourself to be a child of the darkness" (*My Utmost for His Highest*). Victory is realized when we learn to be sensitive to God's Spirit—the Holy Spirit—and to live according to His will and not just according to our desires.

As you complete this study, ask God to open your heart—first, to the love He personally has for you, and second, to those landmines the enemy has strategically placed in front of you.

When you feel as though your resolve is about to give way, remember Paul's words in 1 Corinthians 10:13. Commit to memorize this verse during the course of this study.

Read 1 Corinthians 10:13. When have you personally experienced the truth of this verse? _____

_____

Faithfulness in Disappointment

Most of us know the story of how David was forced to leave his home and family in an effort to escape a sure death at the hands of King Saul—a man who was filled with jealousy and envy. (See 1 Sam. 19–21.) Saul knew that one day David would reign over Israel. He became determined not to allow that to take place. God used Saul's unbridled jealousy to force David to wait until he was ready to become king. Disappointment is an emotional response to some failed expectation or some desire that we have. It is a landmine that explodes with heartache and sorrow.

David, however, prayed, "Be gracious to me, O God, be gracious to me, for my soul takes refuge in You; and in the shadow of Your wings I will take refuge until destruction passes by" (Ps. 57:1). He was learning to live beyond the landmine of disappointment—something that he would practice years before ascending Israel's throne. There is a strong hint of encouragement in his words, and it is something that each one of us needs in our lives. David knew his survival and his future depended on one thing—God's faithfulness.

Read Psalm 139:11-12, written by David. What hope do you find in these verses?

_____

_____

While David did not know the future, he realized that he knew someone who did. You may feel as though your life is a mess. From a human perspective, it may seem this way, but never forget that God—who is infinite in knowledge—can take the most troublesome circumstances and turn them around for good.

**When disappointments come, what do you do?
Check the response that most readily describes you.**

❑ **"Life is so bad. I can never get ahead."**
❑ **"Lord, this is certainly difficult. Please show me how
to respond to the trial I am facing. Help me learn
what You want me to learn through this difficulty."**

You may not understand why your employer said no, why you were passed over for a promotion, or how you will ever reach some of the goals you have set for yourself. How disappointment came into your life is not the issue, but your response to it is. You may be shocked, hurt, angry, or want to run. That's OK. Yet if you cling to any one of these, they will lead you away from God's goodness, and circumstances will become more dismal. An open heart to a faithful God is a foundational step to gain strength and freedom during deep disappointments.

"All discipline for the moment seems not to be joyful, but sorrowful; yet to those who have been trained by it, afterwards it yields the peaceful fruit of righteousness" (Heb. 12:11).

Recall a time when a disappointment ultimately

strengthened your faith in God. _____

_____

The author of Hebrews encouraged us not to give up in Hebrews 12:11 (see margin). We are disciplined or trained by disappointment to trust God with an undivided mind and heart. We conquer disappointment by standing strong in our faith and not wavering through doubt or self-pity. God has promised you victory over the very things that the enemy would use for your defeat—landmines in the path of the believer.

**Write a prayer, seeking an open heart to a faithful God
during life's difficulties.**

_____

_____

The Landmine of Pride

Of all the sins listed in God's Word, pride is the most destructive. Other sins reflect an unmet need in our lives, but pride is a root for many of our sinful thoughts and actions. Satan mistakenly believes that if he can establish a foothold of pride in our lives, he will have access to our minds, wills, and emotions. When this happens, everything changes. Life begins to revolve around our motives, talents, gifts, and desires.

Read Proverbs 8:13; 16:18-19; 29:23. Summarize what you believe these verses teach about pride.

_____

_____

When you are immersed in pride, you rarely consider God at all. Pride arrogantly shouts, "I don't need anything or anyone, especially God, because I can make it on my own." No one is self-sufficient. We need God first, and then we need one another. God created us this way.

In the list printed in the margin, check all that you feel are evidences of pride in one's life. Put an asterisk by those that describe you.

A struggle with pride leads to a selfish attitude; the refusal to listen to the advice of others, a lack of submission to those in authority, a spirit of rebellion, bragging, and even the inability to receive a compliment or gift.

You may ask, "Isn't it right to have pride in my ability? After all, I have talents and I'm smart. What possibly could be wrong with taking pride in the talents God has given me?" Nothing is wrong with having a sense of pride in doing things well. God gives us talents and abilities to use for His

- ❑ Desires to be number one or first
- ❑ Continually refers to oneself
- ❑ Willing to help those less fortunate
- ❑ Longs to be the center of attention
- ❑ Seeks after the praise of others
- ❑ Dresses to gain the attention of others
- ❑ Easily lets others take the credit
- ❑ Needs to be seen in prominent places
- ❑ Has a humble spirit
- ❑ Refuses to apologize when wrong
- ❑ Eagerly helps with menial tasks
- ❑ Has an attitude of self-sufficiency

113

glory, and He wants us to do our best. When we do, we honor Him and His life within us. However, many people fail to honor the Lord with their attitudes. They believe Satan's lies, which tell them they can accomplish whatever they want apart from God. This line of thinking always leads us away from God. And Satan wins the battle.

To the person who has never accepted Christ as his or her Savior, the enemy whispers, "You don't need a Savior. Don't bow your knee to anyone. After all, you're the boss of your life." Believers are not exempt from this type of temptation. It just comes from a different angle: "Don't ask for help. You can do it apart from God. Why tell your friends you are struggling? After all, they will make fun of you and think you are weak."

It doesn't take the enemy long to sense our areas of weakness. He studies our actions and our reactions to life's circumstances. Although he is not omnipotent and could never know us the way Christ knows us, he looks for an opening in our hearts and emotions. Before long we feel tempted to think, *Look what I have done. I have achieved so much in life.* When our thoughts follow this pattern, we yield to his age-old deception—pride.

In the margin, list areas of your life in which you are tempted to be prideful. If you are willing to give those areas to God, make a large X through the list.
Pray, asking God to take away your prideful attitudes and to teach you how to rest in His infinite care.

Don't fall for Satan's tactics. You may think you need to push your way through life, but you don't. Through Jesus Christ you are all you could ever hope to be.

day Four

The Consequences of Pride

When it comes to pride, King Nebuchadnezzar, is a standout. You can find his rise and fall in the Book of Daniel, chapters 1–5.

Read Daniel 4:24-33. According to verse 27, what did God warn King Nebuchadnezzar to do or he would

suffer serious humiliation? _____

_____

According to Daniel 4:30, where were the king's

thoughts focused? _____

In keeping with His nature, God gave King Nebuchadnezzar the opportunity to repent and turn away from pride. By that time, the king was not interested in pleasing the Lord because his life was totally caught up in pleasing himself. When you look at the world today, does this seem familiar? People sin and then angrily cry out to God, asking why He allowed them to be caught up in such tragic circumstances.

However, not all sorrow and adversity come as a result of acts of disobedience. Some of the disappointments come from living in a fallen world. Many come because we have ignored God. Or thinking that we know what is needed, we fail to obey God's commands.

King Nebuchadnezzar became more prideful with each day until his heart had grown cold to the things of God. One of the greatest fallouts from pride is that it alienates us from God. After a year, God did exactly what He said He would do. The king suffered the consequences of his pride.

As you read further about the consequences of sin, ask yourself the questions found in the margin of page 116. Are you setting yourself up to suffer the consequences of your pride?

Pride hinders our fellowship with God. We cannot be loyal to Him and be self-centered and self-serving. (See Matt. 6:24.) If you are more interested in living life your way than you are in pleasing God, then you are dealing with pride, and God will have to remove it.

Pride leads to broken relationships with others. Instead of thinking about what they can do to help and serve others, prideful individuals think

Who is someone you can serve this week, and what will you do for that person?

only about how they can benefit from a relationship. If you think you have done something to create a name or position for yourself, then you may want to reconsider your evaluation because God is the only reason we have life. Take Him out of our lives, and we have nothing of eternal value to offer. If you are serious about removing pride from your life, ask God to show you how you can serve someone else.

Pride blocks God's blessings and often causes us to lose our rewards. Most people tap into just a small portion of the spiritual wealth that God has stored up for them because they are so busy working, striving, reaching, and longing for something more materially. God tells us, "Seek first His kingdom and His righteousness, and all these things will be added to you" (Matt. 6:33). God's blessings offer a sense of fulfillment and peace that you will never be able to achieve on your own. His call to you is to be faithful in what you have been given to do.

In your life, are material or spiritual blessings more important to you?

How can you emphasize spiritual blessings more?

Pride decreases our effectiveness as a leader. Whether you are a leader of a few people, a leader in your church, Sunday School, or a large organization, people want to follow someone they trust—someone who has their best interest in mind. However, prideful leaders fail to see objectives clearly because they are wrapped up in their dreams, goals, and desires. I've seen this at work in the business world and in ministries. Instead of thanking God for the success, a leader steps back and thinks, *People are right. Look what I have done. I'm important.*

Pride entices us to favor people who build up our egos. There is a tendency for the prideful to be surrounded by those who say what they believe the leader wants to hear. If you find that this is true of you, then you need to ask your friends to be honest with you. Are you the type of friend they can call on in times of trouble, or would they say that you think more about yourself than about helping in times of crisis and trouble? Are you a giver or just a receiver?

Where may God be telling you to stop, wait, or slow down today?

Pride sets the stage for us to make foolish mistakes and shuts down the work of the Holy Spirit in our lives. The enemy is waiting for the right opportunity to tempt us to venture away from God's principles with words of pride and self-reliance. Discerning people know the difference between right and wrong. They can sense God saying, "Stop!" "Wait!" or "Slow down!" But the prideful person never gives an ear to God's instruction and runs headlong into trouble, making foolish decisions and reaping the consequences. He will think that he is too smart to need someone else's help or insight; that he can handle everything alone.

Pride breeds prayerlessness. The prideful person does not want to connect with God—through worship or prayer. She may attend church for appearance's sake, but actual devotion is missing. Prayer keeps us in line with God's will. It is only through prayer that we grow to know Him and love Him better each day.

Pride prevents us from experiencing a personal, intimate relationship with the Savior. All the knowledge this world has to offer cannot save you from an eternal death. There is only one way, one God, one destiny. Those who come to Jesus Christ through faith will not perish but will have eternal life (John 6:47; 10:27-30).

Have you made a decision to accept Christ as your Lord and Savior?   ❏ **Yes**   ❏ **No**

If not, are you willing to put away pride and make that commitment today? If so, sign your name below, write today's date, and talk to someone about your decision.

If you desire to dig deeper:

In the acrostic below, for each letter of the word prayer, write how prayer may keep the landmine of pride at bay. For example, for *P*, you might write: "Puts focus on God."

P

R

A

Y

E

R

day *Five*

Successfully Dealing with Pride

The landmine of pride is one of the most deadly weapons in Satan's arsenal, the very one that caused Satan's fall from heaven. When pride holds a prominent place in your heart, Christ is not Lord. Even if you have accepted Him as your Savior, you must choose to turn every area over to Him and allow Him to live His life through you. When you do, He will bless in ways you never thought possible. (See Eph. 3:20-21 printed in the margin of the next page.)

Here is a checklist of steps to successfully deal with the landmine of pride.

1. *Realize that pride is present in your life.* Before God can fully change your heart, you must make a decision to turn away from the very sin that is separating you from Him.

2. *Ask God to forgive you for being prideful.*

3. *Pray that God will give you the ability to turn away from pride.* Ask God for the strength to lay aside any pride that you may have in your life. At times God removes pride by allowing you to face disappointment and even times of brokenness. Remember, though, that He breaks us only in order to bless us. Brokenness is always a pathway to blessing.

4. *Pray that God will set a hedge of protection around your life.* Also, ask for the discernment to detect the landmine of pride before you approach it.

5. *Remember where you came from and how far God has brought you.* Paul admonishes us in 1 Corinthians 6:11 to never forget that Christ died for us—for our sins. Pride beckons us to look down on those who are trapped in sin. Yet God calls us to pray even harder for those who have drifted in their devotion or never made a commitment to Christ.

6. *Ask God to help you recall the good things that He has done in your life, and stop comparing yourself to someone else.* No one else is exactly like you. You are precious in His sight, and He loves you more than anyone possibly can or ever will. When you draw comparisons between yourself and another believer, you open a door for pride to enter.

7. *Be willing to experience adversity.* God does His greatest work in the hard times. Remember that whatever drives us to God is always good for us. When we respond by crying out to Him, a wondrous thing happens: He turns in our direction—opens His arms and draws us close.

Using the seven steps above as a "recipe" for your prayer, write a prayer about the pride that might be in

your life. _____

_____

_____

Before the Session

1. On each of six pieces of poster board write in scrambled fashion one of the following words: *disappointment, pride, jealousy, compromise, fear,* and *slothfulness.* Save for the last week's session.
2. Enlist a learner to briefly recount the life of David, including his disappointments in spite of being anointed king (1 Sam. 16–31).
3. Enlist a learner to briefly recount the life of King Nebuchadnezzar, emphasizing his prideful heart (Dan. 1–5).
4. Bring a clear glass, a sugar cube, and water to class.

To the Leader:

Pray for the learners in your class. Pray that they learn practical lessons from this study about avoiding the landmines that Satan throws in our paths.

During the Session

1. Write the word *landmine* vertically on a board. Challenge learners to think of creative phrases, beginning with each letter in the word, to describe the word. For example, beside the *L* someone might say "leads to devastation," and for the *A* someone might say "annihilates everything in sight." Say: *Just as landmines are an offensive tactic used by enemies in times of war, landmines, according to Charles Stanley, can be spiritual as well. They are strategies used by the Devil to defeat us.* Give several examples of spiritual landmines, such as gossip, unforgiveness, and cynicism, not yet mentioning the landmines that will be covered in this study. Draw attention to each of the six posters, challenging learners to unscramble the words. Say: *These six landmines will be emphasized in this study.*
2. Explain that while the Devil's tactics are difficult, our God is mightier than anything that Satan might toss our way. Call on a participant to read aloud 1 Corinthians 10:13, and invite volunteers to share their responses to the second activity in Day 1. ♥
3. Ask learners to define *disappointment*. After a few responses, read the definition penned by Dr. Stanley: "Disappointment is an emotional response to some failed expectation or some desire that we have" (p. 111). Explain that the landmine of disappointment can discourage us when any adversity hits, even the explosion of other landmines. Call on the learner enlisted earlier to briefly recount the story of David, who had been anointed king but had to wait for years before actually becoming

king. Ask another learner to read aloud 1 Corinthians 11:24-28, which highlights some of Paul's difficult circumstances. State that despite these disappointments and difficulties, God was still faithful to work in the lives of these men to do His will. Invite learners to share when a disappointment ultimately strengthened their faith in God (Day 2).

4. Ask learners why Dr. Stanley calls pride the most destructive sin (Day 3).[It is a root for many other sins.] Form two groups and challenge each group to present a brief role play exhibiting pride. Or, ask learners to share an experience in which pride reared its ugly head. Invite learners to share what they believe the Bible teaches about pride, based on their study of Proverbs in the first activity in Day 3. Call on the learner enlisted earlier to briefly recount the story of King Nebuchadnezzar and his prideful heart. Ask: *How does the world today tend to endorse pride?* Point out that wrongful pride always leads to destructive consequences.

5. Form seven groups, if your class is large enough, and assign each group one of the seven consequences of pride discussed by Dr. Stanley in Day 4. Ask each group to present that consequence to the class, giving either a biblical or contemporary example. If your class is small, lead in a discussion of the seven consequences, asking learners to give examples as described above. Invite learners to add to that list if desired.

6. Ask a learner to read aloud the final statements of the third point on page 118 of Day 5, beginning with "At times God." Ask: *Do you agree or disagree with these statements? Why or why not?*

7. Display the clear glass, sugar cube, and water. Explain that the glass represents our lives and the sugar cube represents pride. Place the sugar cube in the glass. Ask learners to identify the antidote to pride. Listen to their ideas as you pour the water over the sugar cube and watch it dissolve. Explain that prayer is the answer to dissolving pride in our lives. Review the seven steps on dealing with pride as explained by Dr. Stanley in Day 5, emphasizing that prayer is the common thread in each of these steps.

8. Challenge learners to examine their own lives for evidences of the landmines of disappointment or pride. If they see evidence of either, challenge them to begin to take the necessary steps to turn those landmines over to God. Close in prayer.

Landmine of Jealousy

day One

The Truth About Jealousy

Jealousy is a landmine that strikes hard. It has the ability to cause a great deal of harm to our faith, preventing us from enjoying God's richest blessings. Just because we see someone advancing before us does not mean that God is withholding His goodness toward us. He may be simply preparing us for what will come in the future. He wants to bless us, but He also wants to reveal the deeper motivation of our hearts. That was what happened in the lives of Joseph's brothers. The first time they witnessed their father's love for him, they might have cringed. The second time, they might have rolled their eyes in disgust. The third time, they were ready to strike out in frustration and anger. From that point on, jealousy began to build.

Read Genesis 37:2-3, printed in the margin. If you were one of Joseph's brothers, how would you have

reacted to the situation? _____

_____

_____

"Joseph, when seventeen years of age, was pasturing the flock with his brothers while he was still a youth, along with the sons of Bilhah and the sons of Zilpah, his father's wives. And Joseph brought back a bad report about them to their father. Now Israel loved Joseph more than all his sons, because he was the son of his old age; and he made him a varicolored tunic" (Gen. 37:2-3).

You need to remember Satan's primary goal: shift your focus away from God and onto your circumstances. He wants you to become jealous, distracted, and prideful.

In a very real way, the various landmines mentioned in these lessons are connected. The old adage "one thing leads to another" is very true. It also describes the tactical outline that Satan has in mind. He believes he has set up the battlefield to his advantage. If we have a problem with jealousy, we need to know that this is not the only landmine that we will trigger. The flow will go something like this: jealousy leads to envy and envy to anger and anger to fear. The cycle will continue until we become paralyzed or until we turn to God and ask for His intervention.

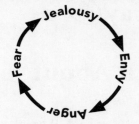

When have you seen such a cycle of landmines in your

life? _____

_____

Many times, the circumstances will not make sense from our perspective. However, from God's vantage point, they make perfect sense. Ultimately He used Joseph's captivity to save an entire nation from annihilation. He used Joseph's plight to prepare him for a very great service, and each one of us is being prepared for a great service.

God loves with an everlasting love, and He has a plan for our lives. This plan, however, may not unfold at the same time as God's plan for another person. We need to be patient and wait for God to give us His blessings at the right time. When we become jealous, we risk missing His best gifts because we are focused only on what we do not have. When we choose this route, a lot of time can be wasted entertaining feelings of heartache, frustration, worry, and envy.

When has jealousy caused you to miss out on some of

God's blessings? _____

_____

_____

day Two

Jealous for Us

When we are jealous, we have made a choice to be envious of others. Becoming hooked by feelings of jealousy means you are out of step with God's plan. While He has the ability to deal with the smaller matters in your life, He never loses sight of His larger plan, which is to draw you into an intimate relationship with Him. Jealousy does not belong in the life of a believer because it goes against the very heartbeat of God.

You may be thinking, *Doesn't God say He is jealous for us?* The answer is yes, but it is a different type of jealousy. God is not envious of us; He is jealous for us, which means He desires our fellowship and love. He has a passionate commitment for us because we rightfully belong to Him and He wants to protect us from evil. Therefore, He watches over us with extreme care.

In Joshua 24:19-20 (see the margin), Joshua's words sounded a strong warning to the nation of Israel not to allow anything in their lives that would hamper their fellowship with God. Over the course of time, Israel's devotion to God waned. It seems impossible to believe, but even after all that God had done for the nation of Israel, they began to incorporate pagan worship into their lives, much to God's displeasure.

"Joshua said to the people, 'You will not be able to serve the LORD, for He is a holy God. He is a jealous God; He will not forgive your transgression or your sins. If you forsake the LORD and serve foreign gods, then He will turn and do you harm and consume you after He has done good to you'" (Josh. 24:19-20).

What in your life tends to hamper your fellowship with

God? _____

How can you eliminate (or minimize) that distraction?

_____

Far too often, we do the same as the nation of Israel by devoting time and energy to the gods of this age—material wealth, social position, and much more. If we do not receive what we think we should, we become jealous, and in doing so we overlook God's goodness and holiness.

Learning to let go of jealous feelings is a process. At some point, everyone has been tempted to envy what another person has. But if we could see what God sees, we would never struggle with this feeling. He tells us it is wrong because He knows it divides our minds and creates an atmosphere of resentment in our hearts. As with all sin, He wants us to acknowledge it to Him and then turn away from it. Israel did not do this. They embraced foreign gods so their devotion to God was divided and they quickly drifted away from Him.

Many believers fight vicious battles with pride and jealousy because they have never fully submitted their hearts to the lordship of Jesus Christ. They hold on to negative, defeating thoughts because they believe if they let go, they will not get what they want. They are rushing through each day with the hope of getting ahead when actually they are falling behind. Whatever is earthly, natural, fleshly, carnal, and demonic does not fit who we are as followers of Jesus Christ.

Often when we are tempted to become jealous, we are afraid that someone will take our place. There is a possessiveness hidden within jealousy that is very dangerous. Even the apostle Peter had to be reminded of this very thing after the resurrection.

Read John 21:20-22. Describe a time when you may have had similar feelings to those of Peter.

_____

_____

Note in the margin any spiritual truths you may have learned from that experience.

Jesus' response in John 21:22 is a perfect answer to the struggle of jealousy—"What is that to you? You follow Me!" In other words, focus your heart on the Savior. Quit keeping score and tallying up nonexistent points. When your eyes are set on Jesus, you will not be concerned about who is getting ahead or who is lagging behind.

From God's Perspective

Jealousy starts inside us—usually with a thought or a feeling that another person has more than we do. Our first inclination is to deny its existence: "I'm not really jealous." Deep inside, however, we look for ways to undermine the other person. We may accomplish this through shutting this person out of our lives or working to turn others against him or her. There is a simple principle we must not forget: we reap what we sow, more than we sow, and later than we sow.

EARMARKS OF JEALOUSY

Comparison. We notice a friend or coworker who has something we want. Or, we see the ability that God has given another person. God knows what we need and what we can handle. He may want to bless us in a certain area, but if He knows we are not ready for the blessing, He will withhold it for a later time. Are you willing to wait?

When the enemy tempts you to compare your ability or life to another, refuse to do it. Turn to the Lord in prayer, and ask Him to help you see your life from His perspective. Though you feel you are insignificant, you are the apple of His eye. Though you wonder whether you are doing a good job, He knows the faithfulness stored up in your heart, and He is blessed by your life. Though there are times when you may feel that you have very little, you actually have great wealth because God does not limit His blessings to material possessions and bank accounts. The love of our families and the valued relationships we share with friends are greater blessings than anything money could buy.

Use the margin to list several nonmaterial blessings in your life. Say a prayer, thanking God for these blessings.

Competition. Whether it is on the job or in your neighborhood, a competitive attitude can breed anxiety, depression, and hopelessness because it tempts you to ask, *Am I as good as or even better than him or her?* The question you really need to ask is, *Am I doing my best?*

Your best will look differently from that of another person. You may never win an award on earth, but you already have the greater reward— the love of God living within you. You have His Spirit, and you can do much more than you think when your heart and mind are set on pleasing Him and not yourself.

I have discovered that when we focus on having more, gaining more, or receiving more, we begin to lose our sense of peace. We become entangled in the world's thought process. In other words, we stop seeing life from God's viewpoint. This is when we begin to worry about our status. We work harder and longer to achieve goals that God never meant for us to chase. We end up exhausted and weary because we are not living in step with Him. We are living with only our self-made goals in mind.

Read Luke 9:46-48. How did the disciples' perspective

differ from Jesus' perspective? _____

How can you apply this spiritual truth to your life this

week? _____

_____

Fear. A jealous person is fearful of being replaced by somebody or something. If God gives you something but does not give me the same thing, what should I do? Many people complain to God, which creates a conflict within their hearts—not just with the other person but also with the Lord. If I am in disagreement with God, then I am in sin.

Strife and dissension are two of the Devil's favorite weapons for war. He wants us to be at odds with God and others. He loves to whisper words of jealousy and condemnation. This is why jealousy is so dangerous. It implies that we are not happy with what God has given us. If Satan can hook us with it, we will move away from God.

Disarming Jealousy

Read Genesis 37:1-11. Rather than plotting against Joseph, how could the brothers have dealt with their jealousy in more constructive, God-honoring ways?

_____

_____

> "[Jealousy] implies that we are not happy with what God has given us."
> —Charles Stanley

How can we effectively deal with the jealousy in our own lives?

First, we need to **admit** that we are envious.

Second, we need to **acknowledge** that we are in conflict with God. As long as we think we can patch up the situation, camouflage it, or rationalize it, we won't deal with the true issue, which is a heart full of envy. Jealousy and envy are listed as sins that are carnal, fleshly, and demonic. In other words, if we continue to practice these sins, our actions are evidence of our lack of love for and devotion to Christ.

Read Galatians 5:19-21 printed in the margin. Circle the "deeds of the flesh" that might be evidenced because of jealousy.

> "Now the deeds of the flesh are evident, which are: immorality, impurity, sensuality, idolatry, sorcery, enmities, strife, jealousy, outbursts of anger, disputes, dissensions, factions, envying, drunkenness, carousing, and things like these, of which I forewarn you, just as I have forewarned you, that those who practice such things will not inherit the kingdom of God" (Gal. 5:19-21).

Third, we need to **thank** God for what He has done in our lives and even for the people who are the source of our conflict. Doing this may seem difficult, but acknowledge your problem, confess it, and thank Him for revealing this struggle in your life.

Fourth, we need to **pray** and ask God to help us see the heart of the other person at the center of the conflict. Jealousy is everywhere—the corporate world, the ministry, the government, politics, your office, and even your neighborhood. You may be jealous of someone who is just being the person God has created her to be. When another person is living God's plan, we never have an excuse to be envious of him or her. Ask God to help you **rest in His presence.** When you learn to sit before Him, waiting for His timing and His direction, you will receive a blessing.

Fifth, we need to be willing to **wait** for God to work. Times of waiting offer wonderful opportunities for us to grow closer to the Lord. As we wait, we also can listen for His voice of instruction teaching us how to live a life that is successful, whether this includes building friendships, working alongside others, or developing new hobbies. Along with waiting comes the need to be open to God's guidance and ready to obey Him at all times in every situation.

Sixth, we need to **ask** God to help us hear His voice over the clamor of the world. Jealousy shouts for attention. Thoughts of envy try to creep into the forefront of your mind. Therefore, stand firm in your desire to hear God's voice and know His mind for your life and situation.

Seventh, we need to **delight** ourselves in God (see Ps. 37:4 printed in the margin). When we do, we find that He will give us the desires of our hearts.

"Delight yourself in the LORD, and He will give you the desires of your heart" (Ps. 37:4).

In the space below, describe a specific situation that may be causing you feelings of jealousy today.

_____

_____

- **Admit**
- **Acknowledge**
- **Thank**
- **Pray**
- **Rest in God's presence**
- **Wait**
- **Hear**
- **Delight**

Look at the list of actions in the margin. Circle the word that identifies where you are in the process of dealing with jealousy in the above situation.

Write down a specific action you will take this week to move further through that process.

_____

_____

_____

Jealousy Toward You

How do you handle the jealousy of another person toward you? The best way is to surrender *your* feelings to God and allow Him to change *your* attitude toward others.

First, you need to **ask God** to show you what you need to learn through this situation. This requires being willing to lay down your own will and desires. Many times people become jealous not because of something we have done but because they feel inadequate or they can never measure up to the standards of those around them. Before a jealous person irritates you, be willing to pray for him, and ask God to help you understand how you can serve that individual rather than shun him.

Second, you need to **make a conscious decision** to ignore any harsh words that have been spoken as a result of jealous feelings. Allow Christ to defend you and also to take care of your reputation. You may not be able to speak truth to a person who is struggling with this landmine, but you certainly can refuse to take a wrong turn—a turn that could lead to destruction.

Third, **ask God to show you** if there is something that you have done to create an atmosphere of jealousy. More than likely, Joseph enjoyed showing off the coat his father had given to him. Jealousy filled his brothers' hearts, and even though their actions were not justified, we can see how Joseph's actions helped to trigger the landmine.

Fourth, show the person who is struggling with jealousy some form of **kindness.** Kindness is a powerful tool. Compliment her. Or make a point to help her in some way. The other person may never know what you have done or may never care. However, God sees your good intentions, and He will bless you, not just for your act of kindness but for the change in the attitude of your heart.

Fifth, **pray** for your attitude to be changed and also for the person involved to focus on the Lord and His purposes. Sometimes, if another person is jealous of you, then the moment you begin to talk with him, you can feel the walls go up. No one needs to become a doormat for others, but we certainly need to allow God to use us and teach us how to have humble, pliable hearts for Him.

Think of a specific situation in which another person

is jealous of you. _____

_____

- Seek God's guidance
- Decide to ignore
- Examine your own actions or attitudes
- Be kind
- Pray

In the list of steps found in the margin, circle where you are in the process of defusing the situation above. Then, write some specific steps you will take this week to move further through that process.

_____

_____

_____

From time to time, each one of us will face temptation in this area and the others mentioned in this study. However, we do not have to yield to any of the deadly landmines the enemy places in our path. Don't allow him or anyone to tempt you into disobeying God. You have been created for a purpose, and that is to glorify the Lord. When you walk through life in step with His principles, you will never be sorry. In fact, life will be fantastic because you will experience His blessings at every turn.

**Read James 3:13-18. Jealousy breeds disorder.
List heavenly wisdom that can combat jealousy.**

_____

_____

leader Guide

Before the Session

1. Draw a path on a poster board or on a chalkboard. Write each of these phrases on a separate note card: *stranger has newer car, coworker makes higher salary, friend goes on nicer vacation, brother has smarter children, neighbor has bigger house, church member has prettier singing voice*. Add additional note cards if desired. Bring extra cards and tape to class.
2. Bring a dictionary to class so that you can read a definition of *jealousy*.
3. Enlist a learner to briefly recount the life of Joseph, emphasizing the jealousy of his brothers.
4. Make a simple bookmark for each participant with the words of Matthew 6:33.

To the Leader:

Continue to pray for the learners in your class. Contact absentees and encourage their attendance. Ask them if they have any prayer requests. Pray for God to reveal destructive landmines in your life.

During the Session

1. Begin the session by telling a story, drawing along the path you prepared as you say: *Once upon a time, a Christian got up in the morning, determined to keep his focus on God and to move faithfully on the path God had for him on that day. He was excited about the blessings God had in store for him. He began the day with high hopes, but then early into his day, his gaze shifted.* Give a note card to one learner; ask him to read the card and tape it to the path. Continue the story: *After that distraction, he continued on his journey.* Stop and give another learner a note card and follow the process above. Continue the story with continued distractions until you get to the end of the path and conclude: *And his day, which started with the best of intentions, ended up not being blessed at all.* Ask learners to identify the landmine that caught this believer in its snare. The landmine is jealousy.
2. Ask learners to define *jealousy*. After a few responses, read a definition from a dictionary. Read aloud the paragraph beginning "You may be thinking" on page 123. Discuss the difference between God's jealousy and human jealousy. Ask a learner to read aloud Joshua 24:22-24. Point out that God's jealousy led the people to a right relationship with Him. Human jealousy creates strife.
3. Call on the learner enlisted earlier to briefly recount the story of Joseph, who endured the devastating results of the jealousy of his brothers.

Form two groups and challenge each group to describe how jealousy might be manifested in each decade of a person's life, beginning with the teens and proceeding through the twenties, thirties, and so forth. Or ask learners to share an experience when they were jealous of another person at a particular point in their lives. From Day 1, discuss the role of waiting on the Lord in defusing the landmine of jealousy.

4. State that jealousy has no place in the life of a believer. Invite a learner to read aloud Galatians 5:22-26 for clear instructions to the believer. Ask: *From your study in Day 3, how would you characterize the life of a jealous person?* Read Dr. Stanley's quotation, "[Jealousy] implies that we are not happy with what God has given us" (p. 126). Allow learners to state whether they agree or disagree with that statement, and why.

5. Explain that with this particular landmine, we can be the one experiencing jealousy toward another person, or we can be the object of another person's jealousy. Form two groups or maintain the groups formed in Step 3. Assign Group 1 the list of steps in Day 4, handling jealousy in our own lives. Assign Group 2 the list of steps in Day 5, handling the jealousy of someone else toward you. Ask each group to review their steps and present them to the entire class creatively and dramatically, such as through song, role play, or pantomime.

6. Lead in a time of silent reflection, perhaps with music playing softly. Ask learners to self-reflect to determine if they are experiencing jealousy toward another person or if another person is directing jealous attitudes toward them. After a brief time of reflection, read aloud James 3:13-18. Direct learners to write a prayer on their note cards, expressing a commitment to God to keep a focus on Him and His many blessings in their lives, rather than on other people. If appropriate for their situation, encourage learners to go to that other person this week and seek biblical reconciliation.

7. Give a bookmark to each learner. Direct learners to read Matthew 6:33 in unison. Challenge learners to reflect on this verse and be keenly aware of God's blessings in their own lives rather than comparing themselves to others. Close in prayer

After the Session:

Mail bookmarks to absentee learners.

Landmine of Compromise

day One

The Truth About Compromise

Like the other struggles listed in this study, compromise will never announce its coming or its deadly intention. And Satan always seems to find a way to use it to his advantage. First, he gains a foothold in a person's life by tempting him or her to yield to his relentless suggestions: "Just once won't hurt. Don't you get tired of being lonely? Don't you want to be part of the group?" Satan always has a goal to reach, and it is to destroy your faith and then your relationship with God.

At some point, each one of us has yielded to compromise—an attitude that develops and grows stronger with neglect and time. At times we think a single choice will not matter, but it does. Compromise reveals a deeper problem with God's principles and the desire to follow after the very things He wants us to avoid. These include activities, choices, and decisions that He knows will bring heartache to our lives and over time erode our faith. Anything that tempts you to abandon what you know is right should be viewed as dangerous and should be avoided at all costs.

Read Genesis 3. How did Adam and Eve's actions

seem inconsequential? _____

_____

The enemy will never caution you to watch your step or to be careful about what you believe. He will never tell you about the deadly power of compromise and its result, which is moral, spiritual, and sometimes physical death. He will taunt you into drifting morally and then applaud your lukewarm decision. Never forget that there is always a small degree of truth tucked away in every one of Satan's lies. This is how he gets us to compromise our convictions and to do the very things God has told us not to do.

How did Satan use a kernel of truth in Genesis 3:4-5 to convince Eve? _____

Compromise prevents us from doing God's will. We miss His blessing because we turn away from His will and take a path other than the one He intends for us to travel. If He has called you to do a certain job, stay at your post until He directs you differently. Even though the situation may be very trying, you will receive a wonderful reward for remaining obedient. If you do leave, you will suffer as a result of your decision. You may experience times of happiness, but the sense of fulfillment will be gone.

Describe a time you did or said something that seemed inconsequential at the time yet resulted in devastating consequences. _____

_____

When we compromise God's truth, we set off a chain reaction of explosions. We could list many social issues that are up for debate today—abortion and homosexuality are two. Both are dead wrong. However, over time, many believers have weakened their stand on these issues. They compromise the principles written in God's Word and ignore the fact that the consequences of their decisions will be devastating for our nation.

Satan knows God will not tolerate sin. Therefore, he wants to trick you into believing you will gain something you deeply desire by ignoring God's principles and doing whatever you want to do. Like Adam and Eve, you come up empty-handed.

Read 2 Thessalonians 3:13. Note in the margin how this verse encourages you to resist compromise.

day Two

A Costly Decision

I remember a time years ago when my son, Andy, and I were swimming in the waters off the coast of south Florida. We took rafts out into the ocean, but because the undercurrent was particularly bad, we kept drifting away. I realized if we were not careful, we would soon be far away from where we had started. I got out of the water and placed a couple of markers on the beach so we would know when we had drifted too far. It did not take long for us to drift past the area I had marked. I quickly realized that we needed to come into shore or we would find ourselves in a dangerous situation.

Compromise usually involves subtle drifting. You know you are moving, but you don't realize how far away from God you have traveled. Warning signals may be going off, but the person who compromises his faith will rarely listen. He just floats farther out to sea.

The enemy always looks for a weak point of entry, and he found it with King David. What began as a seemingly innocent stroll along a rooftop ended in murderous sin. The Bible tells us that when David should have been off fighting battles, he stayed in Jerusalem and ended up compromising what he knew was right before the Lord. He had an affair with Bathsheba and later had her husband killed in battle. Their first son became sick and died. Their second son, Solomon, grew up to become king (2 Sam. 11–12.) After Solomon's coronation, David gave him a serious challenge in 1 Kings 2:3-4. It served as a warning for the future.

Read David's challenge, printed in the margin.
Underline what he charged Solomon to do.
Put parentheses around the benefits of doing so.

Humility marked Solomon's young life. Solomon prayed for one thing: wisdom. (See 1 Kings 3:7,9.) He committed himself to God and went to work building the temple his father David had always wanted to build

"Keep the charge of the LORD your God, to walk in His ways, to keep His statutes, His commandments, His ordinances, and His testimonies, according to what is written in the Law of Moses, that you may succeed in all that you do and wherever you turn, so that the LORD may carry out His promise which He spoke concerning me, saying, 'If your sons are careful of their way, to walk before Me in truth with all their heart and with all their soul, you shall not lack a man on the throne of Israel'" (1 Kings 2:3-4).

for the Lord. People came from far and near to seek Solomon's wisdom, which was godly and just.

Later there was a shift in his devotion to the Lord, and he departed from the godly ways of his father. While there was not a quick turn away from God, something happened in Solomon's heart. That something was compromise. Though he continued to worship God, the intensity and desire for His fellowship changed.

On the surface, the shift may have been barely noticeable. However, buried in a list of accomplishments recorded at the end of 1 Kings 10, we read a single entry that reveals when the devastating change took place: "Also Solomon's import of horses was from Egypt and Kue, and the king's merchants procured them from Kue for a price. A chariot was imported from Egypt for 600 shekels of silver, and a horse for 150; and by the same means they exported them to all the kings of the Hittites and to the kings of the Arameans" (1 Kings 10:28-29). God had instructed him not to associate with other nations, but Solomon did not do what the Lord required. Life began to go downhill for him.

Solomon was blessed in many ways, but he ignored God's Word. In 1 Kings 11:1-2 we also read, "King Solomon loved many foreign women along with the daughter of Pharaoh: Moabite, Ammonite, Edomite, Sidonian, and Hittite women, from the nations concerning which the LORD had said to the sons of Israel, 'You shall not associate with them, nor shall they associate with you, for they will surely turn your heart away after their gods.'"

Many times we think that we can slip away and do something that really does not matter that much. How harmful can it be to do something that appears so innocent? After all, do we really need to be legalistic about everything and everyone?

Solomon's actions were not a problem for other nations. However, for Israel, they were a huge problem, because they opened the door to compromise and sin. If you are involved in an activity and every time you do it or think about it you feel guilty, then you need to know that God's Spirit is warning you that you are standing on a landmine! The spirit of compromise is taunting you to move in its direction. The Holy Spirit shouts, "Stop; don't go there! Don't get involved with it." Unfortunately, we often ignore the warning, yield to sin, and end up detonating the landmine.

Are you involved in any activities that cause you a sense of guilt or discomfort? If so, list those activities in the margin.

What is God trying to teach you? _____

_____

"If you are involved in an activity and every time you do it or think about it you feel guilty, then you need to know that God's Spirit Is warning you that you are standing on a land-mine!"
—Charles Stanley

You won't lose your salvation when you compromise and do the opposite of what you know is right. Yet you risk losing the very thing that has the ability to keep you steady in times of trouble, and that is your intimate fellowship with the Savior. God will not compete with sin. When compromise and sin are present, He can choose to withhold His guidance and friendship until you confess your wrongdoing.

Read Ephesians 1:4 and 1 Peter 1:15-16.

What one word stands out in those verses? _____

Define "holy." _____

What changes do you need to make in your life to live

a holy lifestyle? _____

day Three

Why Do We Compromise?

You may think that you can sin in one area but say no to temptation in another. The truth about compromise is this: it begins slowly and spreads. Once you compromise in the way you dress, you will compromise who you date. If you compromise in what you drink or say, then you can count on easing back on your convictions in other areas. I cannot begin to tell you the number of people who have said to me, "If only I had done what I knew was right." "If I had listened to God, if I had sensed His warning then, I would not be where I am today." We are wrong to think we can take any route other than the one God has called us to follow.

Read Isaiah 53:6. Think how sheep get separated from the flock. How are we like sheep as we begin to

compromise, nibbling on the edges of sin? _____

_____

_____

Let's look at some of the reasons we end up compromising what we know is right:

We experience fear and doubt. Once you open the door to compromise, the enemy begins to taunt your every step with words that are meant to chill you to the core. He wants you to become paralyzed with fear, because he knows you won't go forward if you are afraid.

We want to avoid conflict. Rather than express what they know is right, some people will try to avoid a conflict. They may say, "I don't want to hurt anyone's feelings." Or they may say, "If I say something, I'll lose my job." Instead of addressing the shift from truth to compromise, they will cower and allow things to roll along. If you will seek God's counsel, He will show you when to speak up and when to be quiet.

We have a desire for unity. There are people who do not want to cause "waves." It is always good to seek unity, especially among believers, but never when you end up jeopardizing what you know is right.

We have a deep need for acceptance. Acceptance is one of the reasons people do things they know are not a part of God's plan for them. Ask yourself, "Do I want to be accepted by a group of people who could love me today and not tomorrow, or by an eternal, loving, Heavenly Father, who loves me with an everlasting love?"

We are overwhelmed by peer pressure. If someone tells you that he or she will love you more when you compromise what you know is right, walk away. And if there is a question in your mind regarding right or wrong, wait for God to make His will clear. The enemy will try to tempt you into making a quick, thoughtless decision, but God never will.

We fail to give God what He requires. Many people go to church and worship God but never transfer what they have learned through the teaching of His Word to the area of their finances. Whether we admit it or not, God owns everything. He is the One who gives us the "power to make wealth" (Deut. 8:18). When we fail to tithe and to give to His work, we miss a tremendous blessing. He is specific about giving—it is something we do not want to compromise, especially if we want to obey Him.

We are blinded by pride. People whose lives are riddled with pride may not even think that they are compromising God's truth. They see themselves as being better and more successful, and as having an entitlement to certain things that others do not.

We become spiritually weak and discouraged. When we compromise our basic convictions, our very thought patterns become corrupted. We begin to view life and our circumstances from the world's perspective and not from God's.

Review the reasons above for why we give into compromise. Circle the one most tempting for you. Pray, asking God to forgive you and to strengthen you in this area.

These reasons are why the author of Proverbs admonished us to guard our hearts: "Above all else, guard your heart, for it is the wellspring of life" (Prov. 4:23, NIV). The Old Testament viewed the heart as the hub or the center of the emotions and the will. Today we know that a shift in our thoughts and feelings comes from what we believe, but the principle of guarding our hearts remains true. There is only one way to do this.

"I have hidden your word in my heart that I might not sin against you" (Ps. 119:11, NIV).

According to Psalm 119:11, printed in the margin, what is *the* way to guard against compromise of God's will?

_____

Note in the margin what you need to do to personally gain spiritual strength through the Word of God.

Consequences of Compromise

There is a type of compromise that is useful in business and in situations involving various relationships. We may have an opposing view in some area at work, in our church, or in our neighborhood. Instead of becoming angry and walking away from the situation, we may agree on a compromise in order to get the work done and move forward. It is not sinful. Instead, it is part of our ability to negotiate, cooperate, and work with others.

This was not the type of compromise that touched Solomon's heart. He disobeyed God because he wanted something other than what he already had, and he paid a stiff price for his disobedience. Solomon knew God's commandment. He grew up in David's household and understood the principles of godly living. There were plenty of horses in Israel, but the issue went deeper than material possessions. It struck a cord of sin, which began as an idea of spiritual concession. It was not enough that he had everything a person could desire. Suddenly he wanted his horses to be imported from Egypt—the very place that had once held God's people captive. While he was away from home on a buying trip, the enemy tempted him to become involved with much more than the purchase of a few dozen horses. (See 1 Kings 11:1-2.) Once we knowingly start down the road of sin, we have no idea as to the landmines we will face.

❑ **Your character is weakened.**
❑ **Your personal testimony is diluted and suffers.**
❑ **God's truth becomes irrelevant.**
❑ **People abandon God's Word.**

Look at the list in the margin. Check each one that occurs when you yield your life and heart to the spirit of compromise.

Often nonbelievers are the first to notice a shift in someone's faith. They notice the compromise and make it clear that they are happy you have broken ranks and betrayed the convictions of your faith. Without God, your heart becomes hardened, and you no longer have the foundation of His truth as a basis for your life.

Compromise was a daily problem for the New Testament church. James understood the struggles of believers. He also knew the depth of sorrow and destruction that compromise brings. He asked, "You adulteresses, do you not know that friendship with the world is hostility toward God? Therefore whoever wishes to be a friend of the world makes himself an enemy of God" (Jas. 4:4).

Read 1 John 2:15-17. How can a Christian live in this world without being a friend of the world or loving

the world? _____

_____

We think, *What could be wrong with buying a few horses from another country?* Plenty, if that is what God has told you not to do. To be honest, each one of us has done the same thing at some point. We have thought, *This is so small. I really want to do it. Surely God will approve.* But when He has made it clear that we are not to do a certain thing, no amount of pleading and bending of the rules will work. Obedience always involves a choice: God's way or the wrong way.

When you compromise what you know is right, you lose your ability to act wisely. Living the Christian life requires a lifestyle change that affects every area, from the way we dress to the way we raise our children.

Lot compromised and ended up in Sodom. Abraham compromised and almost lost his wife. David compromised with Bathsheba and lost a son. Pilate compromised what he knew was true and was denied the opportunity to know the Savior. Compromise is costly.

Ask the Holy Spirit to show you in which of these areas you compromise the most. Check all that apply.

❑ **Morality** ❑ **Doctrinal beliefs** ❑ **Marriage**
❑ **Parenting** ❑ **Dress** ❑ **Music** ❑ **Speech** ❑ **Money**

Note in the margin how you can personally begin to turn back toward God in those areas.

day Five

You Can Say No to Compromise

In Day 3 we studied one sure way to stave off compromise. God's Word is your guide to spiritual and emotional healing. A second way is to pray that God will help you restore your faith in Him.

Many times, when people have fallen into sin, they mistakenly believe that they need to do something to gain God's approval. Someone may be thinking, *What I have done is too sinful. God doesn't love me anymore.* There is no sin stronger than the love of God. There is only one thing you need to do and that is to confess your sin and need for God. When you do this, God opens your heart to His love and forgiveness. Faith in God and His ways is the mark of a true believer.

Prayer is an act of faith. It declares our trust in God and in His ability to provide the things we need the most and reflects our desire to submit our hearts to Christ and allow Him to live His life through us.

Read 1 Thessalonians 5:17. Circle the one that best describes your prayer life.

| Almost never | Sometimes | At church |
| Fairly regularly | Constantly | When I am in a jam |

What "sin and need for God" do you need to confess? Talk to God about it now.

If you have never accepted Christ as your Savior, then the first thing you need to do is to come to Him in prayer confessing your need for Him and asking Him to forgive your sin. (See p. 2 in this learner guide.) Talk to your leader about your decision.

As you break your ties with compromise, expect God to work on your behalf. Don't allow the world to define who you are or what you will become. Seek God's approval. Surrender your life to Him, and watch as He removes all the things that once held you captive and replaces them with peace, joy, happiness, and a deep, abiding contentment. This is His eternal promise to you.

Before the Session

1. Gather a black, white, and gray piece of paper for display on the wall and sticky notes and pens for the learners.
2. Enlist a learner to share a testimony about when he compromised his Christian principles and suffered difficult consequences.

During the Session

1. Introduce this study by challenging learners to think of rules or even laws that may seem inconsequential or unnecessary. List these on the board as they are called out. After a few moments, look at each one individually and briefly discuss what may happen if someone disregards the rule. State that today's lesson focuses on the landmine of compromise, which can be detonated when we choose to disregard God's commandments that we may think are unnecessary or that we disagree with.

2. Briefly narrate the story of the original sin with Adam and Eve (Gen. 3). Call on learners to share answers to the question about how Adam and Eve's action seemed inconsequential in the first activity on Day 1. Talk about the devastating consequences. Ask for a modern-day example of a similar experience. (See p. 134.)

3. State that quite often our journey into the landmine of compromise begins with a general drift. Ask for analogies such as the one Dr. Stanley mentions of shifting currents or how a child can wander off and get lost. Ask learners to open their Bibles to 2 Samuel 11 and 12. Briefly review the story of David, who drifted into compromise, only to suffer devastating results. Call attention to 1 Kings 10:28-29 and 1 Kings 11:1-2 found in the text on page 136. Ask: *Although Solomon started strong, in what ways did he drift into compromise?* Invite a learner to read aloud 1 John 2:15-17. Ask: *What were the hooks that lured Solomon?* Lead in a discussion of how we can recognize the subtle drift toward compromise, with one clue being a sense of guilt (as discussed by Dr. Stanley).

4. Display the black, white, and gray pieces of paper on the wall. Guide learners to think of certain "No's" of the Christian faith; there is no question that God forbids these actions. Then discuss certain "Yes's" of the Christian faith; there is no question that God commands His

To the Leader:

Continue to pray for the learners in your class. Ask God to help you be aware of the landmines in your own life and to make you willing to share your experience with landmines with other believers.

followers to do these actions. Write each action on a sticky note and put each note on the black and white pieces of paper respectively. Then explain that we seem often to live in the "land of the gray." The land of the gray is when we compromise our actions. Ask for examples of these gray actions, such as padding your expense account, speeding, being rude to a sales clerk, cheating on taxes, and so forth. Lead learners to discuss God's response to these gray actions. Ask a learner to read aloud Revelation 3:16,19. Then call for responses to the last activity in Day 2.

5. Say: *As we begin the drift to compromise, our journey may be aided by other reasons as outlined by Dr. Stanley.* Review the seven reasons he emphasized in Day 3 and ask learners if they can think of other reasons. Challenge learners to discuss which are most tempting for them. Call on the person enlisted earlier to share his or her testimony. ❤

6. Lead in a discussion about the role of God's Word in enabling the believer to withstand Satan's tactics. Invite a learner to read aloud Psalm 119:11,105. Ask: *How does God's Word equip you to resist compromise?* Allow testimonies of those who have been able to overcome a temptation through using God's Word.

7. Discuss the effect a believer's compromise has on himself as well as on others. (See Day 4.) Read aloud 1 John 2:15-17 again. Hear responses to the second activity in Day 4. Invite learners to share issues that are viable in your community that call for a strong Christian stand. Lead the class to plan ways they can respond appropriately. ☯

8. Read aloud from the second paragraph in Day 5, beginning with the words "There is no sin stronger." Encourage learners that turning to God through His Word and prayer enables us to avoid the landmine of compromise. Invite them to write on sticky notes the areas in which they are most tempted to compromise. Close in a time of silent prayer. Ask learners to toss their slips of paper into the trash can to demonstrate their commitment to living lives of no compromise.

After the Session:

If you know someone who is struggling with the landmine of compromise, pray for that person. Contact that person and offer words of encouragement to stand firm.

Landmine of Fear

day One

A Powerful Weapon

The landmine of fear is a powerful weapon. Like the other landmines mentioned in this study, it has the ability to prevent us from experiencing the blessings of God. However, the landmine of fear takes this concept to an entirely deeper level. It can paralyze us to such a degree that we lose our godly perspective concerning our circumstances. It clouds our vision for the future and leaves us struggling with doubt. When our lives are shrouded in fear, we cannot imagine the goodness that God has for us.

Look at the list of fears printed in the margin. Circle the fears that paralyze you so that you lose your godly perspective. Add to the list as needed.

Read Philippians 4:6, printed in the margin. As you begin this week's study, give your fears to God and ask Him to guide you to trust Him more completely.

David wrote, "Even though I walk through the valley" (Ps. 23:4). Jesus told His disciples, "Let us go over to the other side" (Mark 4:35). God instructed Joshua, "Be strong and courageous, for you shall give this people possession of the land" (Josh. 1:6). Words such as *but* and *what if* do not work with statements like these.

Joshua knew better than to argue with God. Forty years earlier he had seen the results of negative reasoning, doubtful thinking, and fearful projections (Num. 13–14). When Israel first stood at the gateway to the land God promised to give them, fear overwhelmed their hearts. Instead of going in and claiming what God had given, they refused to obey the Lord. What was at the core of their unfounded fears?

- **Death**
- **Illness**
- **Being alone**
- **Financial concerns**
- **Failure**
- **Job loss**
- **Snakes/spiders**
- **Crime**

- **Other:** _____

"Don't worry about anything, but in everything, through prayer and petition with thanksgiving, let your requests be made known to God" (Phil. 4:6).

145

- a lack of faith in God
- a lack of trust in His provision
- ignorance of His presence
- dismissal of His eternal protection
- oversight of His unconditional love

When you ignore the sovereignty and the awesome providential care of God, you will end up struggling with fear. Growing up, I was afraid of the dark. At some point, someone may have said something to me that caused me to feel fearful when the lights were turned out. I remember nights when I went to sleep with the bedcovers pulled over my head.

There came a point when I grew tired of cowering in fear. Whenever I felt fearful, I would pray. If it was dark and I had to deliver newspapers, I prayed for God's safety and protection. Soon fear began to vanish. This one habit helped to set a pattern for my life, which is to get up and pray every morning before I begin my activities. I could never thank God enough for my struggle with fear because it was the catalyst that led me into a closer relationship with Him.

Consider this possibility: God may have allowed you to feel fearful to reveal more of Himself to you.

Recall a time when your fears gave God the opportunity to reveal more of Himself to you. How can that experience prepare you for times of fear in the future?

_____

_____

We struggle with fear because we allow our imaginations to go to places that God never intended us to visit. Most of the events that we fear never come true. Our fears are unfounded. While we worry about impending failure, death, and destruction, Satan is smiling because he knows he has our full attention. Whatever has your attention has you.

In the Book of Nehemiah in the Old Testament, we read how the walls surrounding the city of Jerusalem had been torn down through enemy attack. Most of the people had left or were taken away into captivity.

There appeared to be no hope for rebuilding the walls. Yet God stirred Nehemiah's heart to do the work.

In those days, a wall around a city meant protection and security. Without fortified walls, residents were vulnerable to enemy attack. While Nehemiah went to work on the reconstruction of the walls, his enemies also went to work.

Read Nehemiah 4:9,11-15. Below, circle every action that Nehemiah took in his challenging situation:

Panicked   Prayed   Acted deliberately   Testified Became cynical   Became paralyzed   Became fearful

When you are in a challenging, potentially fearful, situation, how well do you model Nehemiah's decisive

behavior? _____

Notice what Nehemiah did not do. He did not panic, become fearful or cynical, or pack his bags for home. He ignored the enemy's threats because he had been given a mandate by God to rebuild the city's walls.

You may think, *He knew what God wanted him to do.* However, you can know the same thing. God's will and purpose for your life are not hidden. You do not have to guess about the future. If you will pray and seek God's direction, He will provide it.

day *Two*

Consider the Consequences

One obvious outcome of fear is a *divided mind.* The focus of our thoughts is no longer sure and steadfast—set on Christ. Instead, it is fragmented by thoughts of our circumstances, and we find it hard to concentrate on what God has called us to do.

Procrastination is another consequence of fear. People become afraid of not doing something right. Therefore, they put off doing anything! I have listened as grown men have described how their parents told them that they would never amount to anything. Internally they believed this lie, and over the course of their lifetimes they began to procrastinate over the slightest activity. Yes, there was some fear of failure involved, but they also did not believe they could make a choice that was correct or meaningful. So rather than choose, they vacillated between any number of options.

Fear *undermines self-confidence.* It is enslaving and can encompass your entire life. An older man admitted that he had spent his entire life battling an unseen fear. He really did not know how it began, but he knew it was there. He had a low-simmering sense of anxiety that prevented him from trying anything new. As a young man, he believed that God wanted him to enter the ministry, but his parents did not want him to leave them to go to school. Their greatest fear was that God could call him to the mission field and they would have no one. What they had, instead, was a fearful grown man, who had never reached his full potential.

In the margin beside each of the consequences above, write its antonym. Which of these three consequences

of fear above have you experienced? _____

Looking at those two lists, how would you prefer to

be characterized? _____

A NEW PERSPECTIVE

Joshua was a young man when God chose him to take Moses' place and lead the nation of Israel into the promised land. What an awesome responsibility he had been given. It was also a potential opportunity for fear. Moses would not be with him or the people as they entered the land. Israel had a new leader, and he needed to be encouraged and prepared for what was ahead. That was why God instructed him to "be strong and courageous" (Josh. 1:6).

There was only one way for Joshua to accomplish this, and it was by faith in God. If he allowed his emotions or thoughts to turn away from

God, he would become overwhelmed by the task. There are times when we have something that we must do, and the only way to get through it is by setting the focus of our hearts on God and not on our circumstances. There was no way Joshua could lead the people into the land without God's help.

The Lord told him, "Only be strong and very courageous; be careful to do according to all the law which Moses My servant commanded you; do not turn from it to the right or to the left, so that you may have success wherever you go. . . . Have I not commanded you? Be strong and courageous! Do not tremble or be dismayed, for the Lord your God is with you wherever you go" (Josh. 1:7, 9).

Put yourself in Joshua's place. What would have been a normal human response? _____

_____

How does the promise of the Lord's presence help your fears to evaporate? _____

_____

_____

If you want to defuse the landmine of fear, you must change the way you view the issues and struggles of life. You need to ask God to teach you how to view your life and circumstances from His perspective. God wanted Joshua to focus on the following:

- the plan He had for the nation of Israel
- the courage and strength available to him through faith in God

Many times conquering fear is just this simple: when a challenge comes, keep your focus on Christ and not on your circumstances.

Read Isaiah 41:10-13. Use the margin to rewrite God's message to the fearful in your own words.

Overcoming Fear

We begin each day on the battlefield of life. The enemy plants a series of landmines in our path, hoping that we will step on one that will explode and keep us from accomplishing God's will and purpose.

In the space below, write a contemporary scenario of a challenging, fear-inducing situation, perhaps one you have faced recently.

_____

_____

You can overcome fear when you do the following:

• Admit there is a problem and you need God's help. There is something immensely powerful about admitting, "God, I am hurting. I feel fearful, and I know it is the enemy's desire to stop me from being successful. Please help me to hear Your voice and Your words of encouragement."

• Confess your belief in God's sovereign care. Every fear is shattered on a single truth: God is sovereign, and He will not leave us in what appears to be a helpless situation. He has the advantage of knowing all things and seeing every problem or challenge from every angle. He is all-powerful and never hesitates to give us the wisdom we need for every situation. After the crucifixion, the disciples went into hiding. They were sure that they would be arrested for following Jesus and crucified for their faith. Fear tempts us to go beyond a rational point in our minds where we know that God cares for us. Jesus had made it clear that He would have to die, but He would return to them. In the heat of battling fear, they forgot His promise to them and fled (Luke 24:36-39; John 14:3-4,18-21).

• Commit yourself to spending time each day with God in prayer. The single most important activity you can do each day is to pray. Nothing carries the value that this does. Reading and studying God's Word are just as important, but it is in prayer that you learn to worship God and hear His voice speaking to you through His Word and the presence of the Holy Spirit. Each one of us needs to maintain a godly sense of fear. It is a reverent fear for God that reflects our desire to worship, honor, and obey Him. We recognize that He is holy and worthy of all our praise. The psalmist wrote, "O fear the LORD, you His saints; / For to those who fear Him there is no want" (Ps. 34:9). And the author of Proverbs reminded us, "The fear of the LORD is the beginning of wisdom" (Prov. 9:10).

Read 2 Timothy 1:7-11. Describe the difference in fearing God and fearing life's circumstances.

_____

_____

_____

_____

• Meditate on God's Word, which contains His personal promises to you. The truth that is found in the Bible dismantles fear and brings an immeasurable sense of hope. God told Joshua, "Every place on which the sole of your foot treads, I have given it to you, just as I spoke to Moses. . . . No man will be able to stand before you all the days of your life. Just as I have been with Moses, I will be with you; I will not fail you or forsake you. Be strong and courageous, for you shall give this people possession of the land" (Josh. 1:3,5-6). Joshua had this promise from God, and he carried it in his heart. When trouble came, he could remind the Lord what He promised. People who do not read and study God's Word are like ships without rudders. They may be floating, but there is no real sense of direction in their lives. When you have God's Word hidden in your heart, the Spirit will immediately bring a verse of Scripture to mind when sorrow, disappointment, or fear come.

Considering the situation you described at the beginning of today's study, how could you apply one of the four steps outlined by Dr. Stanley to respond in a way that honors God?

_____

_____

day Four

Time to Move Forward

God has given us powerful principles to apply to our lives. He doesn't want us believing Satan's lies that tell us we need to live by chance. There is no such thing as chance or luck in the life of a believer. He knows everything that takes place, and nothing we face is greater than His sovereignty. As children of God, we are living under the canopy of His blessings. Therefore, we are not losers. We are people of great worth because of Jesus Christ.

When we accept Christ as our Savior, God places a seal of ownership on our lives. In the Bible, the word "seal" often was used metaphorically as an expression of something that was held securely. God has given us a seal—the Holy Spirit—as a guarantee of His eternal love. Whenever we feel insecure or tempted to give up, all we need to do is to turn to Him in prayer, and He will provide the hope we need to continue.

Read Ephesians 1:13-19. What encouragement to face fearful situations do you find in these verses?

_____

_____

I remember a time when a group at church opposed me. While I was in a meeting upstairs in the church, the other group was downstairs seeking a way to remove me as pastor. The temptation that came to me was one of worry, fear, and insecurity. I instantly knew that if I listened to these voices, I would not be able to hear God's voice. Therefore, instead of giving in to thoughts of fear, I sought God in prayer, asking for His wisdom and encouragement.

As those around me talked through the things that were happening, I remember being focused on only one thing: God's will. At that moment, He reminded me of the words in Isaiah 54:17, "No weapon that is formed against you will prosper; and every tongue that accuses you in judgment you will condemn." These words contained a powerful message of confidence and hope. It was also a warning not to give up or give in to fear.

> "We can learn to use our fears as stepping stones to a higher level of faith in Christ as we trust Him to guide us, keep us safe, and provide for our needs."
> —Charles Stanley

Read Psalm 27:1,3 and 46:1-2. When you face a serious threat, how can your previous meditations on God's Word help you to remain strong in your faith?

_____

_____

The enemy has one goal for the child of God, and that is destruction through any means he can use. Don't fall for his schemes. If others speak badly about you, keep your heart set on Christ. Do your best and trust Him to be your rear guard (Isa. 52:12; 58:8). We can learn to use our fears as stepping stones to a higher level of faith in Christ as we trust Him to guide us, keep us safe, and provide for our needs.

Think of some of your past fears. How did God use those fears to help you grow in your faith?

_____

_____

_____

Eternal Victory

Some people are so fearful and insecure that they believe if they just try harder, they can earn God's love. But they can't. There is no greater form of love and acceptance than what has been given to you by God through the life and death and resurrection of His Son. The cross is the greatest statement of love and security that has ever been made or will be made.

No one could love you more than Jesus. He loves you—your hair, your eyes, your laughter, your tears, and your smile—all of you. And even more than this, He believes in you. You cannot disappoint Him, because He knows all about you—your sins and failures—and yet He died for you so that you could come to know Him as Savior and Lord and everlasting Friend. What more could we ask to receive than love so great and divine?

The only way to find true peace, confidence, and assurance is to receive the Lord Jesus Christ as your personal Savior. This includes confessing your sinfulness to Him and acknowledging that when He died on the cross, His death paid your sin-debt in full—absolutely and completely (John 3:15–16). The moment you ask Him to forgive you, He does. When you surrender your life to Him, He seals your eternal future with the Holy Spirit (John 14:25–26). This means that while you may face many obstacles, you do not have anything to fear because you are not alone. God has promised never to leave or forsake you (Deut. 31:6,8). Fear vanishes when we apply the truth of God to our situation.

If you desire to dig deeper:

Take time this week to ask the person you named what is his or her "secret" to such courageous living.

Name one Christian you know who lives a life of courage and faith in spite of threatening circumstances.

Say a prayer, thanking God for this courageous Christian role model.

Before the Session

1. List several phobias on a poster board. Use those listed in the margin or find others at *www.phobialist.com*.

2. Write the words and reference for Philippians 4:6-7 on a poster board and then cut it apart word by word.

3. Enlist a learner to briefly recount the life of Nehemiah and his refusal to let fear rule his life (Neh. 4:9,11-15).

4. Type out Isaiah 41:10-13, alternating the phrases between bold face and regular type; photocopy the paper so that all learners will have a copy.

5. Gather enough small, smooth stones and permanent markers for distribution to all learners.

During the Session

1. Begin the session by asking learners to guess the fears represented by the phobias listed on the poster. Some of these may be funny, while others may be more serious. State that everyone has some kind of fear to some degree. If we allow fear to become a landmine, then it can cause us to lose our godly perspective.

2. Distribute the cut-apart words of Philippians 4:6-7 to learners, keeping the first word, "Don't," for yourself. Comment that the Bible has much to say about fear. Two verses in Philippians contain both a command and a promise. Say that the first word of the two verses is "Don't." Tape that word to a focal wall. Call on learners to come up with their words and complete the verses. After the two verses have been completed, read them in unison. Ask for spontaneous testimonies of when God has granted peace to those who prayed about their fears and concerns. Challenge learners to memorize the verses during the coming week.

3. Call on the learner enlisted earlier to briefly recount the story of Nehemiah and his godly courage (Neh. 4:9,11-15). Ask: *What did Nehemiah not do in his potentially fearful situation?* Discuss how fear could have kept Nehemiah from accomplishing the task God had given him. Invite learners to respond to the last question in Day 1 about how well they model Nehemiah's behavior when they are fearful. 🎧

To the Leader:

Continue to pray for the learners in your class. Pray specifically this week that they will acknowledge their fears and give them to God.

Ablutophobia—Fear of washing or bathing
Achluophobia—Fear of darkness
Brontophobia—Fear of thunder and lightning
Coulrophobia—Fear of clowns
Demophobia—Fear of crowds
Ecclesiophobia—Fear of church
Gelotophobia—Fear of being laughed at

4. Invite a learner to read aloud Mark 4:35-41. Ask: *Where was the focus of the disciples?* State that as fears try to dominate our thoughts, we can focus on God to help calm our fears. Distribute the sheets of paper with Isaiah 41:10-13. Lead the class, in two groups, to read the words responsively. After the responsive reading, ask learners to summarize the message of the verses.

5. Maintain the same two groups used for the responsive reading. Direct one group to discuss how Joshua could conquer his fear. Call their attention to "A New Perspective" on page 148. They may think of other biblical characters who conquered fear with God's help. Guide the other group to discuss contemporary examples of courageous Christians. Call their attention to the activity in Day 5. After a few minutes call on each group to report on at least one courageous biblical character and one courageous contemporary Christian.

6. Draw attention to the quotation from Dr. Stanley about stepping stones on page 153. Offer a brief testimony about when God used one of your fears as a stepping stone to greater faith. As time allows, invite others to share their testimonies from the last activity in Day 4. Be alert for testimonies that involve ministry opportunities. Comment that often fear keeps us from serving or reaching out to others. Talk about opportunities for service in your church. Challenge learners to ask God to help them conquer their fears in regards to ministry opportunities either inside the church or in the community. Plan a group project to encourage learners to step out of their comfort zones.

7. State that as we face fearful situations, Satan is often whispering in our ear, "What if . . . ." Yet God is also speaking to us. His words are, in the words of Isaiah, "Do not fear." We must not allow Satan's whisper to drown out the still, small voice of our Lord. Distribute a small stone and a permanent marker to each participant. On one side of the stone, tell learners to write in lowercase letters *what if?* On the other side, tell them to write in uppercase letters *DO NOT FEAR.* Whenever they face a fearful situation, tell them to look at the stone as a reminder of God's presence with them. Close in prayer.

After the Session
Encourage and pray with any learner facing a potentially fearful situation.

Landmine of Slothfulness

day*O*ne

Inexcusable

In 2 Thessalonians Paul wrote to a group of believers who had become lazy in their devotion to God and in their work. Slothfulness or laziness is inexcusable. Before you hesitate to read further because you think this may not apply to your life, ask yourself, *Am I doing my best or do I offer something much less to my employer and coworkers as a result of taking shortcuts and procrastinating?*

> **Circle any area of life where you are tempted to sit back and drift toward laziness until it becomes a habit.**

> **Workplace   Church   Home/Family Relationships**
> **Neighborhood   Society   Relationship with God**

The Bible is very clear about the landmine of slothfulness. It results from a temptation that each one of us will face more than once. Perhaps we have been through a series of disappointments, and our current challenge seems to be more than we can bear. The enemy tells us that what we are facing is much too hard for us. We must stop, lean back, and drop out of life. That was exactly what the Thessalonians did. They stopped working and believing in God's promises.

> **Read 2 Thessalonians 3:6-13. According to verses 7-9, how did Paul lift himself up as a role model of hard**

> **work?** _____

_____

To what extent are you living your life in such a way as to be a worthy role model of hard work? _____

_____

The Thessalonians had become discouraged, and many wanted to give up and quit. Instead of going to the Lord in prayer, the believers became perplexed, worried, angry, disobedient, careless and lazy. They knew God's truth but had stopped living for Him. If we are not careful, we can fall into this same trap.

A slothful person makes up his mind that he does not want to do something, and then he finds a way not to do it. This is a dangerous position. You may be working in an organization that has demanded more of you than you can deliver. Emotionally you are drained. One day you wake up and think, *I'm just not going to do that anymore.* You don't talk about your decision with God. You just decide you are going to check out mentally and physically. *After all,* you think, *it is my life. I can do what I want to do.* But really you can't. By deciding that you will do nothing, you have placed even greater limitations on yourself. And if you do not stop the downward spiral, you will be even more frustrated.

The lame man at the pool of Bethesda is a perfect example. Many who gathered at the pool had no real desire to be healed. They made a handsome living begging for alms.

Read John 5:2-9. What question did Jesus ask the lame man? _____

Christ's question, "Do you wish to get well?" is an important one, because it seems that if the man had truly wanted to be healed, he would have positioned himself closer to the water. Instead, he had spent many years lingering along the sidelines of life. Perhaps he had given up and gave in to the idea of slothfulness.

Jesus always calls the lazy person into action. He called this man to get up and walk. In his letter to the Thessalonians, Paul issued one set of instructions: don't abandon your faith, and get back to work!

For years my mother worked in a textile mill. She never complained about the long hours or the poor working conditions. I was always proud of her. She worked because she had a dream that was greater than our daily problems as a family struggling to make ends meet. Mother had an amazing ability to see beyond our trials to a place of provision. We may not have had much, but what we had was enough. God was enough, and He used those early years of my life to mold my faith in Him. If my mother had said, "I'm not going to do this anymore. I'm tired and worn out. We're going to take handouts from others and get by some way," my life would have been filled with worry and fear. I never would have believed it was possible to come through the storms of life victoriously.

God wants us to look our best and do our best at all times. This does not mean that we will be perfect or that our lives will be error-free. It does mean that we can try to do the very best that we know how to do.

Every landmine we face can be overcome, but not on our own. We need the Lord's help, guidance, and strength. We also need His foresight. He knows what is up ahead in life. We may think we can take time off and just drift for a while, but we can't.

Remember the areas you considered at the beginning of this session where you have made a conscious decision to be lazy or where you are drifting toward laziness. In the margin, write a prayer, giving those areas of your life to God and asking Him to strengthen you to work zealously in that area.

day *Two*

Things to Consider

Have you ever thought about the fact that God is trying to teach you something through your circumstances? He is. He is in the process of training you for a greater work. However, the very thing that can derail His efforts is an attitude of slothfulness.

Read Proverbs 6:9-11. Paraphrase those verses into your own words in the space below.

_____

_____

God expects us to live disciplined lives. A successful baseball pitcher never learns to throw searing strikes by giving up on the game. Instead, he spends hours every day practicing—throwing balls and then watching videos of his performance as well as the performance of others. He is diligent, and he is determined. To defeat laziness, we must be committed to the task and to God. People who achieve success have several things in common: ability, commitment, discipline, desire, and a stick-to-it attitude. They do not give up when life becomes difficult—and it always does.

When we think about it, we discover that the men and women in the Bible each confronted tremendous challenges. Joseph was sold into slavery in Egypt. He ended up becoming a servant in Pharaoh's household and later was accused of something he did not do. In the beginning, Joseph's life was a recording of one injustice after another. However, he did not allow his circumstances to hold him back from being the best he could be. (See Gen. 39–41.)

CHARACTERISTICS OF LAZINESS

- *Lack of priorities, goals, and ambition.* The lazy person will not set goals, because he has no desire to reach them. He lacks ambition and does just enough to get by.
- *Selfishness.* Laziness by nature is a selfish attitude. The lazy person is consumed with his needs and little else. Careless, thoughtless actions carry with them tremendous consequences—if not for us, certainly for those around us. "Me, myself, and I" is the only motto a lazy person knows.
- *Lack of faith in God's call and ability.* The person who has entered this lifestyle may profess to be a believer, but there is no evidence of faith. If there were, he would want to trust God for something better in the future. There is a sense of deadness in the heart and soul of the lazy person that is hard to understand. It is void of true hope, commitment, and faith. Laziness robs us of joy and hope for the future.

**Recall a time when you felt unqualified for a task.
A familiar saying is, "God doesn't call the qualified;
He qualifies the called." How has God proven that to
be true in your life? Make your notes in the margin.**

• *Unfinished tasks.* A person who struggles with a slothful attitude will have a hard time finishing what he begins. He may listen to the enemy's lie that tells him that he does not have what it takes to do the task. When God calls you to do a job, He assumes responsibility to equip you for the task. A lazy person gives up. However, a person who is determined to do what God has given him to do will pray for help and wisdom.

**Write down an unfinished task that is hanging over
your head right now. Commit to finish it.**

_____

• *A damaged testimony for God.* Believers have a keen responsibility to be energetic and committed. Laziness does not fit who we are in Christ. Jesus rested, and there will be times when we need to do the same. But He never withdrew from His earthly ministry for the sole purpose of escaping responsibility.

How can your work ethic help or hinder your Christian

testimony? _____

_____

• *Weakened relationship with God.* When you become lazy in one area, you will be slothful in other areas. In fact, every area will suffer, especially your worship and devotion to God. Lazy people do not think about pleasing the Lord; they think about how little they can do.

• *Ignorance of the truth.* A person who is not committed to Christ will avoid reading and studying Scripture. The enemy tells him it requires too much effort. He can go to church and hear a nice sermon, and that is all he needs to do. We will never mature spiritually or have the tools to combat the negative rebuttals of the enemy if we are slothful in this area.

- *Feelings of depression, anxiety, and fear.* When you forgo reading God's Word, you will not have the spiritual tools to stand against such feelings as anxiety, depression, and low self-esteem. The truth of God's Word is our greatest spiritual weapon. It is our only offensive weapon against Satan's arsenal of negative, slothful words.

day Three

Overcoming Laziness

You do not have to fall victim to any of Satan's schemes. You can overcome this problem when you understand the following.

God has created you for a purpose. He loves you, and if you will trust Him, He will set up the circumstances so that you can enjoy every moment.

What do you believe is God's purpose for your life?

_____

_____

You are not powerless. A spirit of laziness will tempt you to think you will never be free. Jesus tells us, "If you hold to my teaching, you are really my disciples. Then you will know the truth, and the truth will set you free" (John 8:31-32, NIV). Once you accept Christ as your Savior, His Spirit—the Holy Spirit—comes to abide with you. There is no greater power available than the power God's Spirit provides. However, you must appropriate His strength to your life.

God has a plan for your life. In Jeremiah 29:11, God assures us: "'I know the plans that I have for you,' declares the LORD, 'plans for welfare and not for calamity to give you a future and a hope.'" Lazy people wait for someone or something to drop into their lives. They want an easy ride with no form of commitment. But true joy comes when we decide to take God's challenge and begin a walk of faith with Him. Will you trust Him enough to get up and walk toward Him, believing that He wants to give you a future that is more than you dreamed possible?

How, specifically, does your life give evidence that you are trusting God with your future? _____

_____

Where do you need to trust Him more? _____

_____

God forgives sin. God stands ready to forgive your sin and to give you the wisdom and strength to overcome this struggle with slothfulness or any other sin. However, you must seek His forgiveness.

He is your only source of victory. You are in spiritual warfare, but there is no need for you to lose this battle. When your faith is firm in Christ, He will fight for you and provide a way out of this bondage. Life's greatest foe is no match for God's Son.

Read Psalm 18. Describe how God is your:

Rock _____

Fortress _____

Stronghold _____

The Lord is also your Deliverer, who sets you free from the bondage of sin. He has overcome the world, its passions, lusts, and fears. More important, He has overcome the enemy. Satan is a defeated foe. You do not have to take one single step toward any of his landmines.

Encountering Landmines

No matter the landmine—disappointment, pride, jealousy, compromise, fear, or slothfulness, there are two ways we encounter landmines. The first is by *taking a route that God does not want us to travel without knowing the consequences.* Many times, we make mistakes. We may sense God warning us to be careful and not take a wrong step, but we do it anyway, thinking that maybe we will be okay.

I left In Touch Ministries one afternoon a little before two o'clock, and I was sure that I had plenty of time to keep a three o'clock appointment. But as I stopped at a traffic light near the expressway, I caught myself wondering which way I should turn. At that moment, I sensed God's Spirit saying, "Don't go that way—don't get on the expressway."

One of the ways we avoid landmines is by heeding His directional guidance. On this day, however, instead of heeding His warning, I headed straight onto the interstate and into traffic! Before I reached the bottom of the entrance ramp, I realized I had made a huge mistake. Traffic was backed up as far as I could see.

Someone reading this may ask, "Is God really interested in something as minor as traffic on I-85 in Atlanta? Does God really speak to us this way?" The answer is yes! God wants us to know that He is actively involved in all we do. He speaks to us through His Word, through the Holy Spirit, who lives inside us, and through godly counsel. When your heart is turned toward Him, you will sense His voice directing and guiding you through every situation.

When a landmine explodes, we immediately turn to the Lord and seek His forgiveness. His grace sufficiently covers us in such times. This does not mean you will avoid all of life's traffic jams, heartaches, and disappointments, but it certainly does mean He will be with you every step of the way—guiding you, leading you, and answering your prayers.

The second way we encounter landmines is by *making a choice without any consideration of God.* Our passion and desire to reach our own goals supersede what we know is right, despite the consequences. Every day we make countless choices—some include important decisions, while others on a human scale may seem minor.

From God's perspective, some of the smallest decisions are the most important because they reveal our true nature and character. This is why you should tell the clerk at the store when he gives you too much change. And it is exactly what our children and peers need to witness overflowing from our lives, a desire to be godly and avoid landmines, even the small ones that can be just as deadly as the large ones.

Many times we fail to consider God's might and powerful love for us. We don't take time to think about His personal promises. Instead, we mentally rush past evidences of His faithfulness; dismiss His ability to heal, provide, and restore; and move forward without consulting Him about the future. When we make a conscious decision to bypass God and His principles, we make a horrendous mistake.

Which of the two ways we encounter landmines is

most problematic for you? _____

If you desire to dig deeper:

Think of other promises of God that guide you in your decision making.

_____

_____

Look up the following passages and make note of how God's promise can guide you in making decisions that will help you avoid encountering landmines.

Philippians 4:19 _____

1 John 1:9 _____

James 1:5 _____

Deuteronomy 31:8 _____

day *Five*

Someone to Guide You

"I couldn't help myself," one man, who was involved in a relationship with a woman other than his wife, told me. He was a believer, but he stepped on the landmine of sexual sin. "Oh, yes, you could," I replied. "You have the ability to say no because Jesus Christ lives within you through the presence of the Holy Spirit."

What simple principle is found in Proverbs 3:5-7 that you can use to avoid the trappings of Satan?

_____

You can go to church every Sunday and still end up hitting a landmine if your life is not submitted to God. Living for Christ involves a heart commitment and not just a personal performance.

Even though you may choose to sin or step away from God's will, His love covers you (see 1 Pet. 4:8, printed in the margin). He does not agree with or support your sinful actions, but He never stops loving you. And when you turn back to Him, He forgives and restores the relationship you share with Him as your Savior, Lord, and loving Heavenly Father.

"Above all, keep fervent in your love for one another, because love covers a multitude of sins" (1 Pet. 4:8).

Now you know what landmines are, where they are located, and how to avoid them, the question you will have to answer is, how will you handle them? The road you are on does not have to lead to an intense combat zone. You can learn to spot the landmines that the enemy places along your way and avoid serious injury.

Read Psalm 37:23-24. How does this passage encourage you as you strive to avoid Satan's landmines?

_____

NOTES

Before the Session

1. Get a long sheet (about 6 feet) of freezer paper, tape, and several markers. Label the sheet of paper with the words *Promises of God.*

2. Get two poster boards. On one write the words of Proverbs 3:5-7. Save the other for Step 4. Gather the posters created during Week 1.

During the Session

1. Begin the session by asking learners to identify an animal they think epitomizes hard work and why. Then ask them what animal epitomizes laziness and why. Next, ask which of the two most represents their lives, acknowledging that there may be a little of both in all of us. Point out that the final spiritual landmine to be discussed is slothfulness or laziness. Ask learners for any honest reactions to this week's topic. While this may not be commonly considered a sin, God's Word points out that laziness clearly is not a pattern God intends for His followers.

2. Call on a learner to read aloud 2 Thessalonians 3:7-9. Discuss how Paul clearly identified himself as a role model of hard work. Lead learners to discuss how they are living their lives in such a way as to be worthy role models (Day 1). State that being a role model of hard work extends beyond the workplace and into other areas of our lives, such as our relationships, neighborhoods, church and society. 🔊

3. Mention Joseph's life from the material on page 160. Explain that Joseph easily could have given up and given in to slothfulness. Ask learners to think of other men and women in the Bible who displayed a strong work ethic when they could have had an excuse for giving up. [If learners struggle, suggest Paul, Peter, Moses, Noah, and Nehemiah.] Lead in a roundtable discussion of how a Christian's work ethic can help or hinder his or her Christian testimony, encouraging learners to share their responses from Day 2, page 161. 🖤

4. Ask: *Do you believe laziness is always a conscious decision, or can one drift toward laziness until it becomes a habit?* Allow responses. Lead the class to review the list of characteristics of a lazy person identified by Dr. Stanley in Day 2, and then challenge the learners to reword the characteristics using the letters of the word *slothful.* Write the word

To the Leader:

Continue to pray for the learners in your class. Pray specifically this week that they will examine their lives for any signs of laziness and will commit to allow God to work in them to rid their lives of this landmine. Continue to pray for and encourage learners whom you know are struggling with landmines.

NOTE

vertically on a board. Describe a characteristic beginning with each letter. Then, challenge them to describe the opposite of that characteristic, writing the opposite out to the side. Note that this list of positive characteristics would describe the biblical characters discussed earlier. Lead learners to reflect on how well these descriptions fit them.

5. Conclude the session on slothfulness. First, call on a learner to read Jeremiah 29:11. Affirm that God has a plan for each life but in order to live that plan we must fulfill our part. Call on a learner to read aloud 1 Peter 5:8-9. We must remain firm in our faith and actively resist the Devil. If we allow the landmine of slothfulness to explode in our lives, we may very well miss out on some of the amazing blessings that God has planned for us. Ask learners how the points in Day 3 encourage them to combat laziness.

Landmines discussed in this study

Disappointment
Pride
Jealousy
Compromise
Fear
Slothfulness

6. Conclude by reviewing the six landmines discussed during the study. Point to the poster of each landmine as you mention it. Describe the two ways we encounter landmines as described by Dr. Stanley in Day 4. Encourage learners to share which way is the most problematic for them from the first activity in Day 4. Be sensitive as learners share. Stop to pray for those willing to open up with their colleagues.

7. Spread the long paper and markers on a table. Invite learners to come to the paper and write the promises of God that guide them in making decisions (Day 4). After a few minutes, tape the paper to the wall and review what has been written. Allow participants to read some of the verses that are meaningful to them.

8. Direct learners' attention to the Proverbs 3:5-7 poster and lead them to read the Scripture in unison. State that keeping our focus on God will help us to avoid the landmines that Satan places in our paths. Ask: *How can you appropriate God's strength for your life?* Lead learners to recall Dr. Stanley's emphasis on meditating and knowing God's Word, spending time in prayer, and waiting on the Lord.

9. Ask learners to open their Bibles to Psalm 18. Suggest they offer prayers of praise and thanksgiving to God using Psalm 18 as a basis. Give everyone who wishes an opportunity to pray; then close the prayer time.

10. Distribute the next issue of *MasterWork*. Announce Beth Moore's study in the Book of Psalms, *Stepping Up*. Ask the learners to complete the learning activities in Week 1 before the next meeting.